"From the first pages it is evident .... p........ ....,
and what is more, Vandermeulen is a skilled writer adept in presenting material in
small digestible morsels that will maintain your interest."
   —*Norman Goldman, Editor of Bookpleasures*

"Vandermeulen provides lots of motivation; she makes you truly believe that you
can 'conquer all obstacles'!"
   —*Tanya Guerrier*

"Great tool! It's great to have so much information in one place."
   —*Dana Taylor*

"The best how-to book I have ever read ... Jo-Anne's voice and bright smile came
through the text on every page ... It does not matter if you are promoting a book,
a business, or an upcoming special event, you have got to get this book to help
you get the word out to millions of people in a very cost effective (free) way."
   —*J Renaud*

"A real time saver! Jo-Anne lays it all out in a clear, concise format."
   —*Tracy Krauss*

"I have to admit, I was not getting my hopes up on this one. I started with the
sample today. Very impressed. It is worth investing."
   —*Najia*

"Gaining exposure on the Internet has never been so easy! ... The huge marketing
benefits from this book are astounding."
   —*Brian Knight*

"Page after page of fantastic ideas. Heck, I found myself not just reading it to
review the book, but taking notes so I could apply her secrets to my own career."
   —*Duncan Long, Internationally Recognized Technical and Fictional Writer
      with Over 70 Books in Print*

"Jo-Anne has another winner!"
   —*Deborah McCarragher*

"Ms. Vandermeulen's clear, concise approach makes the almost mystical haze of online marketing easy to grasp for the most neophyte of Internet users. And just to be sure, she includes a very good glossary in the back of the book to help you understand strange, almost ethereal concepts such as 'tags' and 'blogs' … And I can promise you one thing … I'll be keeping this book close by for years to come!"
  —*James Holloway*

"If you are spinning at the thought of promoting your book or product or service, this book will plant your feet on the ground and point you in the right direction. The ideas here apply to everyone with a product or service to market."
  —*Katherine Kane*

"Jo-Anne Vandermeulen provides a wealth of information and services for writers. I've learned a lot by simply reading her material. Her advice is sound, and her energetic promotional efforts world class."
  —*Donald Jeffries, Prolific Poet (Songwriter), Novelist of Sci-Fi/Fantasy and Children's Literature*

"[Jo-Anne Vandermeulen] takes the mystery and guesswork out of book promoting, freeing a writer time to write!"
  —*Stuart Ross McCallum, Author of "Beyond My Control – One Man's Struggle with Epilepsy, Seizure Surgery and Beyond"*

"An absolute waterfall of information! Well done."
  —*J. W. Nicklaus, Author of "The Light, the Dark, and Ember Between"*

"… so much good info here. I'll be coming back to read more."
  —*G W Gresham, Author of Thriller Fiction*

"Great info … I've tried to explain this same concept so many times. It's not hard to apply, and I know you have helped a lot of people with your excellent information. Thank you for that."
  —*Adrienne Smith, Good News Merchant*

INTERNET MARKETING EXPERT

Jo-Anne Vandermeulen

PRESENTS

INTERNET MARKETING
Made Easy

Massive Internet Exposure Guaranteed!

*Practical Marketing Ideas To Create
Massive Exposure And Drive Traffic To
The Site Where Your Products Are Sold*

www.premiumpromotions.biz

LAURUS BOOKS
WWW.LAURUSBOOKS.COM

I give credit and thanks to all of the bloggers and marketing experts who have generously taken time to share their wealth of knowledge with others like me.

INTERNET MARKETING
Made Easy

By Jo-Anne Vandermeulen

Paperback Book ISBN: 978-0-9826957-0-8
E-Book ISBN: 978-0-9826957-9-1

EDITED BY: Nancy E. Williams and Diana L. Meadows
COVER AND LAYOUT DESIGN: Jennifer Cappoen, Nancy E. Williams

PUBLISHED BY

LAURUS BOOKS
POST OFFICE BOX 894
LOCUST GROVE, GEORGIA 30248 USA
www.TheLaurusCompany.com

PRINTED IN THE UNITED STATES OF AMERICA

This book may be purchased in both paperback and eBook from LaurusBooks.com, Amazon.com, and other retailers around the world.

INTERNET MARKETING
Made Easy

Are you searching for practical Internet marketing ideas, presented in a user-friendly fashion? Welcome to "Internet Marketing Made Easy."

> **A "must-have" resource book filled with practical online marketing tips for those who have products to sell.**

Each section highlights valuable content, showing you exactly how to market on the Internet so you can be successful.

Sections:
- Blogging – *Getting Started, Creating a Following, Establishing A Voice, Advancing in the Search Engines (SEO), Jo-Anne's Favorite Tips*
- Social Networking – *Guaranteeing Massive Exposure*
- Creating A Platform – *Attracting Clients*
- Targeting Your Audience – *Saving Energy*
- Balancing Online Activities – *Managing Time*
- Reaching Your Goal – *Success, Here I Come!*
- Glossary – *Popular Internet Terms Used in This Book*

Create relationships on the Internet. These are the first "words of wisdom" that I share with those who ask me how I became successful. Being proactive on the Internet is a must, and it is imperative that you have a *blog*. A blog is a website indicated by the link, http//www. A blog is used for highlighting you and your products.

Think of your blog like a booth at an exposition. Others wander over to your station and have the ideal opportunity to really get to know you and what you are selling. There is no pressure. You are not dragging them over or holding an advertising sign in their face. Internet marketing is fun—a win-win for both you and the viewers. You present your passion, and they become interested in what you have to sell.

Isn't it much easier to sell a product when there is trust? Can you not sell more if your friends share your link with others? You are no longer marketing on your own, and selling has suddenly become easier, all because creating relationships on the Internet is building a HUGE friend or follower list. These hundreds and thousands of followers become your advocates. They constantly share endorsements for even more to come over to your blog.

> *The marketing tips in this "must-have" resource book can be applied to any products you may wish to promote via the Internet.*

Whether you are a novice or an expert, **Internet Marketing Made Easy** is the book for you. I guarantee you will take away valuable content that will save you time and energy when marketing on the Internet.

—Jo-Anne Vandermeulen

Acknowledgements

⸺◦⬦◦⸺

*T*his book would not have been possible without God's grace. He has given me a second chance. Never take things for granted. What is here today can be gone tomorrow.

> *"Losing an ability doesn't have to be a devastation. I have learned to conquer all obstacles, to count the blessings, and to hang on tight as the momentum increases and takes me on a journey I could never have imagined."*
>
> —Jo-Anne Vandermeulen

A special thanks to the following:

My editor, publisher, and dear friend, **Nancy E. Williams** with *The Laurus Company*, as always turned this manuscript into a work of art. Nancy edited and designed the page format to turn a non-fiction resource into an easy sight on the eyes (pun intended). Her editorial skills are top notch, too.

Special thanks also to co-editor, **Diana L. Meadows**, for suggesting that we include the Glossary. This has been a great help for Internet marketers.

My business partner, **Brian Knight**, is another necessary appendage to my life—always around to steer *Premium Promotional Services* in the right direction when I'm unavailable. His easy-going demeanor is so necessary when I'm frazzled. He is a man with a genuinely HUGE heart.

YOU! This book is possible because of you. Your words of encouragement, support, and shared knowledge fuel my body, giving me the energy necessary to gain speed. God bless you all.

PLEASE NOTE

A list of **popular Internet terms** that are used in this book, along with their definitions, can be found in the **Glossary** beginning on page 111.

As an additional aid for our readers' convenience and under-standing, these terms are underlined and **footnoted** at their first appearance in this book.

Table of Contents

BLOGGING – Getting Started

BLOGGING – Creating a Following

BLOGGING – Establishing A Voice

BLOGGING – Advancing in the Search Engines (SEO)

BLOGGING – Jo-Anne's Favorite Tips

SOCIAL NETWORKING – Guaranteeing Massive Exposure

CREATING A PLATFORM – Attracting Clients

TARGETING YOUR AUDIENCE – Saving Energy

BALANCING ONLINE ACTIVITIES – Managing Time

REACHING YOUR GOAL – Success, Here I Come!

GLOSSARY – Popular Internet Terms Used in This Book

About the Author

Blogging

—∞∞∞—

GETTING STARTED

To Blog or Not To Blog, That is The Question

*W*hat are the advantages of <u>blogs</u>?

1.   **Multi-Functional** – A blog can work as a website. A tab at the top of the blog site can guide the viewer to your business or personal website.

2.   **User Friendly** – You feel more in the driver's seat. A blog is easy to create, and you can do it yourself with no <u>HTML</u> skills. You don't need software or an expensive web designer.

3.   **Timely** – By updating regularly, you can stay current with the "needs" of your audience.

4.   **Interactive and Personal** – <u>Blogging</u> is a great way to stay in touch with your readers in a more informal manner. The audience is involved by submitting comments. You can generate a following with this connection, discover what they want so you can delve into the requested direction of their interests or concerns, and YOU get more exposure through marketing yourself and your product(s).

Blog: An interactive Internet site. A term shortened from "weblog," a type of website for journaling in chronological order with newest posts first, usually by one person, with the option of allowing comments from readers.

Blogging: Maintaining a blog, or making a post to a blog.

HTML: HyperText Markup Language, the predominant computer language (code) for building web pages.

5.   **A Showcase of Your Ability** – You write, and they read for themselves your awesome abilities, style, and voice.

6.   **Free** – Many blog hosts are free.

7.   **Higher Search Engine Exposure** – More exposure for you. Using links and tabs, each keyword will pop up in search engines.

8.   **Easy to Maintain** – Free and quick assistance is available from expert technicians, if needed. They will provide answers to any questions and solve any concerns.

What are some of the popular blog platforms?

I would need to be experienced in many different blog platforms to recommend the best. I use Wordpress for "Conquer All Obstacles," but we have chosen Blogger for "Premium Promotional Services." Popular blog platforms are:

- Wordpress
- Blogger
- Typepad
- Tripod
- Squarespace

What kinds of things should I have on my blog pages?

You must ask yourself: What type of blog do I want to write? For me to *conquer all obstacles*, I want to promote myself. My blog has:

First Page, Feature Page, or Home Page

What you want as your focus will determine your first, or feature, page. Walk in the shoes of your target audience. Use updated posts with information your followers will find useful.

Blog Platform: The software used to create blogs, the most popular being Blogger and Wordpress.

Links: A highlighted or activated word, phrase, or address that, when clicked, will direct the viewer to another URL or site.

Pages, Blog: Multiple pages of a blog site. Clicking on the tabs (usually found at the top of the pages), will direct the viewer to different pages. Common pages include: Bio, About, Reviews, Contact.

If you want to promote your product(s), make sure you add a picture of your product on the <u>sidebar</u> of each page, or feature this as your first page. (Note: Wordpress does not allow you to advertise, so you may want to use Blogger as your blog platform if you are selling a product.)

You may even decide to have your bio, a synopsis, or <u>pitch</u> as your first page. You have control of the steering wheel. The key to promoting yourself or your product is to understand your customers and their buying habits.

Make sure your blog welcomes Comments and that it is easy. First impressions are lasting impressions. People need to trust you before you pitch your product. This is why I recommend making the advertising about your product separate from your feature page.

Sidebar <u>Widgets</u>

I recommend the following widgets on your sidebar, from the top down:

- A friendly and professional photo of you. Link the photo back to your bio page.
- A <u>badge</u> your followers can click to <u>subscribe</u>, with easy to follow instructions: "Click here for your FREE bi-weekly subscription."
- Your product photo. Link this to another page where you can detail information—About/Price/etc.
- A search space. I use Google Search, plus my own search button for easier navigation.

Badge: An image displayed on a blog or personal profile on social media sites that identifies you. Most badges encourage readers and followers to download and display their badge on their followers' site or blog and to link back.

Pitch: A short paragraph or verbal conversation that is intended to hook buyers for the product(s) you are hoping to sell.

Sidebar: The smaller columns to the left and/or right of the main center column on a blog page. Typically, widgets and a variety of links and information of the blogger's choice are added to the sidebars.

Subscribe: To request to receive messages posted to a mailing list or newsgroup, or notification via email of new posts on a blog. The presence of a Subscribe button on a blog enables the blogger to acquire a database of email addresses.

Widgets: Small applications (programs) you can add to your website or blog. Includes icons, pull-down menus, buttons, selection boxes, progress indicators, on-off checkmarks, scroll bars, windows, window edges (that let you resize the window), toggle buttons, forms, and many other devices for displaying information and for inviting, accepting, and responding to user actions. Widgets are usually found on blog sidebars. There are hundreds of widgets to choose from. These widgets dress or add personality to your blog. For example, a widget will allow you to add images or pictures.

16

- List of Blog Rolls
- List of Groups to which you belong
- Categories. List 3-5 only (Change the term "Category" to "TITLE," as viewers are more receptive to this term.)
- List of Recent Posts
- List of Resources
- Archives
- Recent Comments
- Meta or Log In button
- Subscribe RSS button. (This is very important, so you can link your other blogs together.)
- Blog stats. (This is questionable.)

Bio Page

The most viewed page will be your bio page. Sell yourself. Present an eagerness to talk about yourself and your work.

- Write in third person.
- List facts not wishes.
- Cite relevant information.
- Write tight. Limit to three to four sentences.
- Add a <u>hook</u>.

The four questions your viewers want answered from your bio:

1. Who are you?
2. What is your expertise *(can they trust you)*?
3. How does your expertise address their problem or goal?
4. How can they contact you?

- DO keep your professional bio as short as possible.
- DO be selective; DON'T list your entire professional background.
- DON'T be bland; let your personality show.
- DON'T include information that isn't relevant to your audience. *(However, DO remember that viewers like to get to know the REAL person. For example:* "I love walking Oscar [a mini-dachshund who has my unconditional love!]" *will show authenticity, which is also what followers are searching for.)*

Hook: The first sentence that grabs a reader's attention.

Contact Page
Promotional Page

Are the dynamics of my blog appealing?

Make everything look user friendly and attractive. Do not clutter the page. More does not necessarily mean better.

- Use a white background with black print. Keep it simple. No fancy flashing buttons, music, or slow to download animations.
- Remember, your audience is there to read your material, and they don't have a whole lot of time. Give the reader what they are looking for right away. The fewer times they have to click to find what they want, the greater the chances they will stick around.
- Give cohesiveness to each page—same format and structure.
- View other sites and ask yourself why you like or dislike their pages. Nothing wrong with borrowing ideas.

How do I get people to find my blog?

People will discover your blog through:

- **Search Engines** – The goal is getting your name listed at the top of the search engines. You need a brand, <u>keywords</u> repeated often in your title, content, links, and <u>tags</u>.
- **Marketing** – Constantly post your "signature" everywhere: in forums, blog comments, and emails.
- **Promoting** – Promote your site. Advertise by updating your status in <u>Social Media Sites</u>, such as Facebook, LinkedIn, Twitter, Google+, and Goodreads (especially if you're an author). Promoting can be

---

Keywords or Key Phrases: A blend of words used in your title and content depicting the content. The purpose of using keywords and key phrases is to aid the search engines in matching information that is typed into a browser search bar with information in the search engine databases.

Search Engines: A program for the retrieval of data, files, or documents from a database or the Internet. You can find others, answers, and/or products. Examples of the top three search engines include: Google, Bing, and Yahoo. Approximate Market Share: Google–79.19%, Bing–9.03%, Yahoo–8.79%, Ask–1.66%, AOL–1.32%.

Social Network Sites: A community on the Internet where individuals register to become members, supply their profiles, accept and send friend requests to gather their own following or fans. Popular social network sites today are Facebook, Twitter, and LinkedIn.

Tags or Meta Tags: HTML code found in the "head" area of a web page that contains: (1) a description of the content; and (2) keywords informing search engines about the page.

time consuming and must be done constantly to be effective. If you are tight with deadlines or want to focus solely on other pursuits, you may want to consider paying someone to build your platform and promote your product.

Successful Blogger = Really Love Thy Neighbor

The characteristics of a successful <u>blogger</u> are not too far off from the attributes of an excellent teacher. I taught school for twenty years and swimming for five years before that. Classroom management was my strong suit. The fact that I loved my students made them love me in return. I can honestly say that I was a great teacher, and I truly had wonderful students.

Having a teaching background has helped me become an expert blogger in a short amount of time, but that is not a requirement. Don't worry if education is not in your background. You may still have the essential qualities to *conquer all obstacles* and become a blogger with a huge following. Ask yourself these questions:

Can you captivate an audience?

Whether it is one-to-one or in front of a group, are all the eyes cast upon your face and anticipating your next words?

Write articles in a variety of ways. Include various instructional methods because your audience will be made up of all levels of learning. They will be at different stages. Presenting a variety of methods and complexity of content is so important. When I write a <u>post</u>, I sometimes use point form or questions, bold statements, and quotes. I usually include examples. Hook your audience right from the beginning. Repeat what works and draws responses.

Blogger: Someone who makes posts to a blog. Also, the bloghost, blogger.com.

Post: An entry made to a blog.

Are you sincere when you show that each individual is special?

Accept all attitudes. The viewer must feel included and part of a community. They will not only want to stay until the end of the post, but they will come back to read more. Begin the post with a welcome. Be inviting for the newbies by encouraging their talents. Invite them to guest blog and offer to guest blog on their site. Thank the followers and fans. Really show your appreciation by telling them that without an audience, you definitely wouldn't be a blogger. You need them ... tell them that. Your viewers are needed!

Is your message positive and the new content attainable?

Present content in positive messages—"do" instead of "do not do." Keep the negative words out. Instead of using the word "never," use "always." As a lifeguard, I would call out to a running child to "walk on the deck." I did not use the words, "don't run." The word "walk" is positive and shows the behavior you expect and need for them to understand. Yelling the words, "don't run," is negative and plants the negative seeds. Words are powerful, so check the phrases you are using in your posts.

For your viewers to respect you, you must first genuinely respect them.

Blog the Net, Surf the Wave of Positive Vibes

*W*riting is subjective. What one person loves, another may hate. Yet, there are ways to write in order to draw in your targeted audience. This "target" is what you must aim for to be a successful blogger, attract new viewers, keep existing readers coming back, and even sell your products.

How do I become a successful blogger?

1. **Research.**

How do your competitors draw their HUGE following? Borrowing ideas (not copying) is smart. Learn from those who are successful. Look for:

- Eye-Catching Titles or Headings
- Photographs or Images *(See Copyright Infringement on page 61.)*
- Valuable Content: Topics – Relate To Your Audience – What they are searching for – key words that draw and hold their attention
- Presentation is Everything: Mix formal language with conversational-style posts

2. **Really Know Your Audience.**

Where do they go to mingle or, perhaps, to purchase their products?

- Blogs
- Forums
- Social Networking Sites

3. **Know when to pitch and when to back-off.**

There is a fine line between advertising and spamming. "Where can I go to buy that?" versus "being a nuisance."

4. **Remember your past clients.**

Already-earned trust is priceless. Past clients are the key to promoting to others. Re-marketing: It is a lot easier to re-sell an existing customer than to search for new ones. Give, give, and give again.

5. **Check your stats.**

What is working to raise your stats, and what isn't working?

More heads are better than one. Instead of seeing other marketers as competitors, work together as a team, and watch for amazing results. Attitude will determine your success. View your journey as a challenge, not as an obstacle. Your "voice" will ring true in your writing. Have fun. Others will want to jump aboard and surf the net, the wave of positive vibes.

Social Networking: Developing relationships by conversation, whether in person or online, that grows into a trusting bond through interactive connection—becoming friends.

Spamming: Unsolicited commercial messages sent via email, or forwarded emails.

Stats: Short for "statistics." Stats show the number of visitors, their locations, how they got there, and how long they spent on each page.

Turning First Impressions Into Loyal Followers

*I*t can be a challenge to get your first time visitors to return to your blog/website, but it doesn't have to be. *Conquer all obstacles* by evaluating your site with THIS CHECKLIST:

❏ Make the subscribe button accessible. Top side widget, label with clear instructions.

❏ **Occasionally remind your readers to subscribe.** Don't assume anything.

❏ **Produce an attractive blog/website design.** Make your site reader friendly—KISS.

❏ **Add personality and engage your readers.** Use informal language, add pictures, invite viewers to contribute. They will want to journey with you.

❏ **Revisit stats and analyze data.** What topics/posts generate the most traffic? Capitalize on strengths.

❏ **Promote on social media sites.** "Connect with Jo-Anne," then list sites you belong to, and your viewers can follow (ie: Facebook, Google+, Goodreads, MySpace, Gather.com, etc.).

❏ **Link to past posts.** New followers will appreciate direction.

❏ **Give.** Readers are searching so give them what they want.

❏ **Be consistent and keep the content fresh.** Keep a schedule and post formats the same.

❏ **Find key players.** Encourage friendship. Opportunities will pop up.

❏ **Post great content.** Engage your readers, form a sense of community where readers feel they belong.

KISS: An acronym for "Keep It Simple, Sweetie," or Silly, or Stupid.

Blogging

CREATING A FOLLOWING

Today's Bloggers Must Be Convincing!

Wouldn't it be heaven to have all your readers respond, "Gosh, I need to continue reading this!" "Ah, now I understand!" "I can do that!" "So cool!" "Definitely worth the read!" "That is easier than I expected!" *(heavy satisfying sigh)* "Wow, I never knew that before!"

Think about an article you struggled to finish reading. Or, when was the last time you actually paid full attention to an advertisement?

E-Notes' *Encyclopedia of Business, Advertising*[†] states, "Many managers believe that an ineffective advertising campaign simply won't return a meaningful sales increase, but there is evidence that certain ads have actually diminished sales. When segments of the public find an ad irritating or when ads deliberately or inadvertently raise negative concerns, consumers may avoid the advertiser's product or service. In addition, some ads may draw attention to an entire product category, thereby benefiting competitors as much—or more—than the advertiser."

E-Notes continues: "Among measures of effectiveness, whether before or after an ad is run, those related to persuasion tend to be most valued. This relates in part to the basic selling proposition: if it's a strong proposition, the ad is more likely to persuade; if the underlying proposition is weak, no amount of creativity in the execution will change people's minds. According to some advertising veterans, the ability to shift consumer attitudes far outweighs the benefits of simple name recognition and similar effects."

[†] E-Notes "Advertising: Encyclopedia of Business" (www.enotes.com/biz-encyclopedia/advertising)

TODAY'S SUCCESSFUL BLOGGER'S CHECKLIST

Does your TITLE:

❏ *convince the reader that what you have to offer is essential and needed now, with a sense of urgency?* Don't forget to hook the reader with a killer title. Only 20% will read farther than the heading, so sharpen those barbs and use the finest bait possible.

Does your CONTENT:

❏ *match the title?* Check the entire post and then re-evaluate the working title.

❏ *deliver inclusive and realistic information?* Use examples proven to work for you by sharing experiences.

❏ *offer credibility?* Provide examples/quotes/stats/reports/testimonies.

❏ *show "uplifting" conviction?* Encourage the reader with realistic content and attainable goals.

❏ *engage the reader?* Use lists, and spice up the tone by blending facts with a sprinkle of stimulating conversation.

Does your FINISHED POST:

❏ *express the amazing content in a concise format?* Edit by cutting unnecessary words.

❏ *show uniqueness and professionalism?* Be genuine. Misleading the reader even a bit will lead to disastrous results. Not only will they stop reading, but they will never return. Fresh bait always works better than rubber worms.

❏ *emit quality?* Carefully tuck keywords throughout the article without sounding staged.

Functioning Link: When a link works to connect to another URL (internal page or external site). Ideally, that external site connects back with yours, so that you are sharing traffic.

❏ *provide simple direction for action?* Explain in "layman's terms" what the reader must do next in order to get what they're searching for. Provide <u>functioning links</u> or buttons with clear explanations.

❏ *end with a bang?* A strong ending will quench the thirst, leaving the reader satisfied, feeling their time was well spent.

When the blogger produces an irresistible post, the viewers will:

- Acknowledge and appreciate the importance of the written content.
- Read the entire post with full attention.
- Take action by investing their time/purchasing the product.

Today's blogger must be convincing in order for the reader to be dedicated to reading more and to keep coming back. Using this checklist will help you *conquer all obstacles*.

Become a Blogging Expert Overnight

*W*ith age comes wisdom ... but not when we are talking about blogging. It does not take years to become a blogging expert. You can *conquer all obstacles* and become a professional as early as tomorrow. Yes, I said *tomorrow*.

To become a blogging expert, all you need to do is:

- **Define Your <u>Niche</u>** – Mental blocks will be unheard of. Never will you tire for what you're passionate about. Mental juices will flow. The articles will ring true—with an honest voice. The reader will devour your post.

- **Carefully Proofread** – Checking for the usual punctuation and grammar is a given. Beginners can ask someone to look over their article. Swapping articles—having a critique partner—is an excellent idea.

Niche: A certain interest group toward whom you will focus your efforts. Your area of expertise. Thoughts should come easy when you're writing about your passion.

- **Content Must Give** – Producing valuable content will attract new readers and have viewers coming back for more.

You are now ready to attract a **LARGE NUMBER OF READERS**, but the competition is fierce. Tons of blogs are out in the Internet. A lot of those blogs are filled with valuable content. **So how does a blogger stand out from the rest?**

Fact: *"The Internet is a vast wasteland of thoughts and ideas. According to Technorati, someone creates a new blog every 1.4 seconds. If blogging was a crime, and in some cases it very much should be, it would be the number one source of criminal activity in the land."*

— Adam Brown, FreeLanceSwitch Site, 01/07/09

Before pushing the submit button to have your post published, ask yourself these questions:

Who are my readers?

- **Gender**

Words and expressions will be different depending on your audience. A title for a majority male audience will likely be different from one targeted for a female audience. For example:

Male = Sex, Battle, Respect

Female = Love, Solve, Nurture

Can you think of other words that are used depending on gender?

- **Age**

Think about the age of your audience. Writing for young adults requires a different style than posting for a senior-age audience.

Check the Feedburner stats. Facebook Business Pages now give you a complete profile of your audience—gender, age, geographical location, and the number of views over the week.

If you are not happy with the facts, then it's time to change your vocabulary and style based on your audience.

Am I writing for viewers or Search Engine stats?

- **Check the title.**

Every now and then, I will write an eye-catching title, rather than words-only terms with <u>key phrases</u>. I am still getting comments from my blog post titled, "Who Likes To Get Naked?" I'm pretty sure the search engines did not pick this title up, but it sure attracted readers.

The title "8 Tips To Successful Blogging" was successfully picked up by the <u>web crawlers</u> but would have easily been skimmed by those who were uninterested in improving their blogging skills.

What is the main purpose for my blog?

- **My blog post must be clear to my audience and true to myself.**

Create your title and article to reflect your purpose. Whether you have decided your posts are for interaction, to help or inspire others, to build friendships, or to sell products, keep your promise by staying on task and resolving the questions before the end of each article.

You can *conquer all obstacles* and become an expert blogger, but you have to follow some guidelines that have proven successful when publishing posts. There are many blogs that supply tips and techniques to assist bloggers in becoming stronger. Research and read what has worked for other experts. Toss that fear out the window. Write the posts, and then check the stats. You never know, a new vocabulary and style of writing may be a better way to go and the answer as to how you can become an expert blogger overnight.

Key Phrases: A blend of words used in your title and content depicting the content. The purpose of using keywords and key phrases is to aid the search engines in matching information that is typed into a browser search bar with information in the search engine databases.

Web Crawlers: A computer program that browses the World Wide Web creating a copy of all the visited pages for later processing by search engines. This new content will boost your site higher in the Search Engine results. This strategy is called Search Engine Optimization (SEO). For example, being page ranked 3 means that the viewer will only need to scroll to page 3 in the search results to find you—pretty high ranking compared to the thousands of pages that exist.

Content is the Key

*Q*uality matters! Enhancing your followers' lives will gain you respect and credibility, and it will produce even more followers.

You have a keychain full of keys. They are heavy, pulling down your arm, and jingling as you step. A closed and locked door is in front of you. This door is your blog, and there is only one key that will work to unlock the barricade, the solid wall that's obstructing your view.

Which key will open the door?

1. An impressive title
2. Optimized search engine links
3. Consistent posts
4. Great content

If you chose #4, you have discovered the main key to opening the door. So now you step into the room, and what do you see?

You see a room crowded with followers. You notice that they are becoming a tad restless, thousands of heads looking around, eyes darting for the nearest exit. They obviously don't have time to stick around. *Oh, no, they're heading for the doorway.* Quick, you must act fast!

How do you keep your audience from fleeing?

No! Don't shut the door and lock them in. No one likes to be trapped. Don't throw your content at them. No, don't keep what you know a secret. Instead, please them with your great charm. Use your voice that gives you elegance and a sense of wholeness about the message that matters the most to you. Smile and relax into the content that brought your followers into the room in the first place. Now is the time to prove your credibility. You have to earn their respect.

Ah, I have their attention now. Good.

Invite your guests to sit down. Pour them a glass of wine. Now is the time to show an interest in them. Interaction is a must. Ask questions, make direct eye contact and respond back. Heck, they may agree to link your blog with theirs.

Your followers have come to your blog for a reason. They are in your room because of the great content you've provided in the past. They are hungry, needing to devour information that they can use. So, serve your guests the fine food you've been busy preparing. Present your delicacies on a silver platter. Let them choose which ones they want to taste. Choice is good. Let them decide on the amount of cream cheese they wish to scoop up on the cracker.

If you have provided quality content, your guests will probably talk about their experience after they leave. Can't you just see them sharing with their friends their memories of the fine wine and fabulous food they received in your room ... oh, ah, I mean your blog? ***Word of mouth, or <u>viral promotion</u>, goes a long, long way.***

> *To *conquer all obstacles*, the most important key to opening the door of success is to produce a blog with great content.*

Give your followers what they are searching for. Don't hold back. Yet, be careful. Your content must be current and researched thoroughly. The information must be accurate. Remember: Quality matters! Enhancing your followers' lives will gain you respect, credibility, and produce even more followers.

Viral Promotion: A strategy in which a marketer creates a campaign focused on the goal of causing viewers to spontaneously spread it by sending it to friends. A form of recommendation.

Professional Blogging

H *ow do I create a blog that *conquers all obstacles* and stays out of the slush pile?*

> *"The Internet is a vast wasteland of thoughts and ideas. According to Technorati, someone creates a new blog every 1.4 seconds. If blogging was a crime, and in some cases it very much should be, it would be the number one source of criminal activity in the land."*
> —Adam Brown, FreelanceSwitch Site, 1/7/09

With these alarming statistics, how do I create a blog that will cause viewers to choose mine to read?

Answer: I must present a professional blog!

I have supplied checklists and information on blogging that will guide you in creating a fabulous site. But check to see if you have "little foxes spoiling the vine." Have you overlooked some obvious "little foxes" in your posts? The following points will cause your blog to appear unprofessional and will push your audience away.

Read the following points carefully and give a check if you can answer affirmatively. Unfortunately, all it may take to turn your viewers off and away, never to return, is for one of these points not to receive a check mark.

❑ *Do I properly type in caps and lower case?*
- Do not take short cuts.
- Do not capitalize your entire title.
- Do not leave everything in bold print.
- Do not leave words like "I" in lower case.

❑ *Do I use the word "blog" correctly?*
  Do not call your post or article a blog. You CAN, however, call your post a "blog post."

❏ ***Do I list two or three "related posts" at the end of my posts?***
Do not include a string or list of related posts. Keep it simple.

❏ ***Do I spell names correctly?***
If they are worth quoting, they are worth respecting.

❏ ***Do I keep my content short, specific, and relevant?***
Avoid rambling.

❏ ***Do I take blogging seriously?***
Readers are looking to you for sound advice.

❏ ***Do I stay up-to-date and keep my readers informed?***
Technology and the world wide web are changing constantly. Be sure you change with it.

❏ ***Do I use pictures to spice up my posts?***
One picture can be worth a thousand words.

❏ ***Do I establish myself as a source of information?***
Develop, and keep, a good reputation. Check out the facts first and follow through with everything.

❏ ***Do I keep my posts positive?***
Bad mouthing and constant complaining is just plain unacceptable.

> ***"Remember, as the medium becomes more and more mainstream, there will be more and more blogs and more and more opportunities."***
> —ProBlogger, Darren Rowse

In the corporate world, your professional blog may soon be seen as a reference tool. The content and presentation of your posts honestly exposes your expertise and can open the doors for many new opportunities, opportunities in areas you may never have dreamed.

Do you want to be a part of this industry? You can *conquer all obstacles* and open the doors for opportunities by blogging professionally.

> *"If you can establish yourself
> as the blogging expert in your niche, not just a
> blog writing expert in your niche, there is money
> to be made from a fertile market."*
> —ProBlogger, Darren Rowse

Why Sex is Important

*O*ne of the first and most effective methods of attracting readers is with your title. And now that I have YOUR attention with the title above, let me offer this advice ...

Do NOT disappoint or totally turn your title into a false "hook." No one likes to be taken for a fool or feel they have been tricked. Stay on topic, carefully weaving the title in and out of the valuable content.

"Why Sex is Important" is understanding how our way of thinking may vary from that of the opposite sex—knowing which personality traits are valuable in producing awesome posts or articles.

Be prepared to reinvent yourself. Your personality trait voice will naturally come through. The usual opposite gender trait may take some conscious effort to incorporate, but it is plausible and can be conquered.

Usual "MALE" Traits: analytical, problem solvers, assertive, logical, authoritarian.

Usual "FEMALE" Traits: good listener, makes friends easily.

(Note: Not all men or women depict these personality traits.)

Individualized Traits: These are traits to which many people aspire: persistent, precise, compassionate, intelligent, attentive, patient, planner, positive, self-disciplined, diligent.

Three Ways To Become A Highly Effective Blogger

1. **Study and understand yourself.**
   Which personality traits come easily and are often portrayed through your voice.

2. **Learn the skills and traits that are used habitually by most expert bloggers:**
   - Write every day – Take time for precision.
   - Edit – Cut the fluff and get to the point.
   - Know your audience – Analyze the <u>traffic</u>.
   - Love to learn – For fresh content read what's new.
   - Remain focused and be consistent.
   - Plan ahead and follow it.
   - Be persistent and positive.
   - Be self-disciplined and diligent.

3. **Make a conscious effort to blend masculine and feminine traits to into a balance skill.**

   How many of these skills come naturally to you? Are you into the same habits as the expert bloggers? To become a successful blogger, incorporate the habits of expert bloggers; know why sex is important in understanding the different personality traits; and blend all traits into your posts.

Traffic: The number of visitors to a blog or website. Your audience, followers, or fans who travel around your site clicking on the links to read more about you or your products. To determine your amount of traffic, go to your stats page.

Blogging

———⟨∞⟩———

ESTABLISHING A VOICE

A Unique Voice Attracts Readers

*H*ave you ever tasted an undercooked cake with no icing? Yuck! Expecting immediate results by presenting articles or posts filled with only facts will leave a bad taste in your mouth as well. Instead, present yourself as a chef, and set some tasty morsels before your guests. Let them feast on your amazing articles or posts. Today's top bloggers have one thing in common—a unique voice. So show off your remarkable voice. Think of expressing your opinion as the icing on a cake, the sweet topping that stands out from the others. Now think of the procedure and ingredients. Blend the egg whites with the icing sugar.

Your post is a mixture, or combination (like cake batter), of formality (straight facts) with informality (conversational style). Adding the delicious icing will totally change the taste of the cake. Your readers will digest the facts in a new way, and they will want to come back for seconds.

But wait ... you're not finished ... a cake needs time to bake, and it must have the correct temperature in order to rise. Over time, your online presence through the social networks will grow, and your products will sell.

If you are a newbie, have patience. Throw "instant gratification" thinking out the window. Close that oven door, and let it bake. Learn to lower your expectations for instant results. Do not expect overnight high traffic stats or massive sales.

But don't worry ... you will *conquer all obstacles* and produce a scrumptious product once you accept that you're in this business for the long run. And with your change of attitude, driving persistence, and proactive participation, your <u>platform</u> will rise, the traffic will increase, and your product will sell.

Totally YUMMY!

Blogging – A Delicious Post Devoured in One Bite

H *ow do I combine great needed content and infuse my post with perspective and background to make it real for the reader?*

Too many writers who blog only serve a plain, dry, fried hamburger patty. Sure, it will attract the hungry viewers, but once they are full, they will wander away. Unless they are starving, chances are they will never return. They will probably discover a better meal down the road.

I can eat a fried hamburger patty, but I find it rather bland on its own. If I add mustard, onions, a few spices, and a bun, I will enjoy the taste much more. Like published posts for your blog, it takes more than good content to entice the reader.

> *Your post must be relevant, fresh, and creative to give the zing that readers are searching for and the smart solutions to their significant problems.*

Liven up those taste buds. The trick to creating a tasty post is to mix the ingredients—blend the meat with the spices to create a delicious meal.

Great food and fabulous company! What else could a person want? Oh, I almost forgot the conversation. Dinner just wouldn't be dinner around my house without the usual table talk. **Readers want solutions they can talk about.**

That fried hamburger patty is the meat the reader wants—the facts and smart solutions to their significant problems. Sprinkle in the spices,

---

Platform: Where you tell the world about yourself and your products or services. Building a personal, reputable identity is essential in Internet marketing. Stand out from the rest.

and you will have added in personality and style, the fun and interesting content to stimulate the brain. Now, you can serve the meal with love, rolling in the respect and care the reader deserves. The conclusive message will stimulate the reader's true appreciation and have them coming back for second servings.

By taking six dry and very important facts, you can create a delicious post and *conquer all obstacles*. In just one bite, your reader will devour your post and be left feeling full and very satisfied.

The Six Ingredients to Successful Blogging

THE MEAT:
1. Good content

THE SPICES:
2. Relevant information
3. Fresh perspective
4. Creative presentation
5. Smart solutions
6. Interactive with great conversation

If All Else Fails ... Laugh!

Your content doesn't have to come across as boring. Writing articles in your blog doesn't have to be daunting. I've already discussed the importance of:

1. Sticking with the topic of your niche.
2. Keeping the format short and sweet.
3. Mixing the writing style from conversational to formal.
4. Creating valuable content.
5. Posts that make you laugh.

Now, think of something funny ...

The last time you read something that made you laugh, did you walk away? One of the most popular status updates on my Facebook <u>home page</u> was a one-liner, fill-in the blank: "I know when I've been on the Internet too long when I _____ ." Here are a few of the many responses:

I know I've been on the Internet too long when I ...

- send an email to myself.
- hit CUT instead of COPY.
- hit the REFRESH button, hoping to wake up. *(Thanks to Nancy Williams from Laurus Books—my publisher.)*

There's nothing better than a good laugh. Writing humor is a gift, and I envy all who can deliver content in a funny fashion. What a fabulous way to hook the viewer and keep them within your post or article. So, if you are one who can get people to laugh, even if it's only an inkling of humor, I encourage you to use it.

If you are more like me, one who has problems remembering jokes and one-liners, use the tools at your disposal. It's okay to save a file of "funnies" you have heard or to use a quote from someone else—with recognition, of course.

How about selecting a photo that made the corners of your mouth turn up? Did you giggle when you saw what I really look like when I've been on the Internet too long? Even tossing in the odd chat acronym (lol) or funny face (:/) can add a light touch to your article.

You can *conquer all obstacles* when you add humor to your posts by using the tools that are available and giving them a touch of imagination. Relax and enjoy the process. ;)

> *"Stopping a piece of work just because it's hard, either emotionally or imaginatively, is a bad idea. Sometimes you have to go on when you don't feel like it, and sometimes you're doing good work when it feels like all you're managing is to shovel sh-t from a sitting position."*
> **—Stephen King**

Home Page: The landing page, feature, or first page the viewer sees when arriving at your blog or website. New blog posts will appear here, along with the generic sidebar(s) as seen on all of your additional pages.

Social Bookmark – Get Noticed Now!

I am going to share a **HUGE TIP** that will allow you to **Hit Over A Hundred <u>Social Bookmarks</u> With Just One Click** (okay, make that three clicks).

But, first, there are some **VERY IMPORTANT DETAILS** that must be in place to ensure optimized search engine success.

Update your <u>profile</u>.

Search engines gobble up <u>keywords or tags</u>. The web crawlers will snag your name and the specific topic you're promoting as long as you have completed the following details:

Detail #1: Completely filled in your profile on search engines, such as Google, Yahoo, and Bing.

Log in at:

> Google – https://www.google.com/accounts/ManageAccount
> Yahoo – http://profiles.yahoo.com/
> Bing – http://www.bing.com/webmaster/SubmitSitePage.aspx

Others should be able to search for you easily. Your followers can enter your name into these three popular search engines and discover your site location and the updated content you have posted on your blog. Optimize the search engines. You must do the footwork. After this, you can sit back and let the "feelers" do their job.

Detail #2: Update your profile in your social media networks.

Example: Facebook/MySpace/LinkedIn/Google+/Goodreads, etc. This may seem like a lot of work, but it is well worth it. Usually, the first place your curious viewers will search for more information about you is in your

---

Keywords or Tags: A word or phrase that BEST describes the subject or article. When searching for an article, what you would type in the search engine to find it.

Profile: The personal information about yourself that you provide during registration.

Social Bookmarks: A method that stores and organizes keywords or tags to ensure optimized search engine results.

profile. Take the time to post a picture, share your interests, and make sure you include links back to your main blog/website. This is the perfect place to display your product with a short description. Be inviting and encourage your viewers' feedback.

Detail #3: Announce your new content.

Twitter, Facebook, and Google+ are simple social media networks to submit a short announcement about your new post. Include the specific link so your viewers can have direct access back to your blog/website. This will be attractive on their homepage as they will be able to view the illustration you have chosen to publish with your article.

On other social media networks, such as NING, make sure you click the RSS feed on the side widget and type in your site address. Your published posts will appear automatically on your profile page.

Hit Over A Hundred Social Bookmarks With Just Three Clicks

Social Bookmark your new published posts. First, ping/bookmark/tab your original published page on your blog/website. Second, go back into your social media networks and social bookmark the page again. The web crawlers will go crazy with excitement and feature you even higher in the rankings.

These three **social bookmarks** save me tons of time and energy:

- **http://www.pingmyblog.com/** – Copy and paste your new page into the "Blog URL box" and give your page a title. Click on the bottom box that says, "Check All," and, boom, you have now hit over 70 social bookmark sites with just one click.

- **http://feedshark.brainbliss.com/** – Again, go through the same procedure as above. Click the "Enable Submit Button," and then click "Submit Now – Chomp, Chomp, Chomp", and, voila, you have now hit another 36 social bookmarks with basically a couple of clicks in one shot.

Address (Web): The URL or location of a site on the Internet. The address bar is usually found at the top of your browser and begins with http://.

Ping: A utility used to test the delay between or to generate a response from one computer to another on a network or the Internet.

RSS Feed: Rich Site Summary, commonly called Really Simple Syndication, is a format for delivering regularly changing web content.

URL: Uniform Resource Locator, the "address" of a web page. The link to your site (begins with http://) found at the top of your browser.

- **http://pingomatic.com/** – The more consistently you post, the more excited the web crawlers become. Realistically, I cannot afford to dedicate all of my time to blogging, so I post two new articles with solid content per week. So where do I spend most of my time?

Do I social bookmark every article on every page?

Yes. This is where I do spend my time, and it's worth it. Going out and setting the crawlers in motion creates immediate results. My name and topic soar to the top of most search engines. (Just type "Jo-Anne Vandermeulen" or "Conquer All Obstacles" into the search engines—Google/Yahoo/Bing—and see where I am. Am I on the first page? You bet! Heck, I may even be #1. :)

So what's my secret?

No secret, really. Here's the procedure:

1. Create a knock out post with awesome content.
2. Send out bursts of short announcements to my friends/followers who are now fans on Facebook, Google+, and Twitter.
3. Encourage any visitors who come to the site to sign up for a FREE subscription. Automatically, new articles will show up in their email.

My followers love it! And you know what this means ... they will share their wealth of knowledge with others, just as I have done. They will tell two friends who will tell two friends who will tell two friends, and so on and on and on.

Good luck and remember ... YOU can *conquer all obstacles*.

Blogging – The Best Post

*C*ompare writing the best post to an *elevator pitch*—**amazing content** with **impressive presentation** in **concise format**.

Cyberspace is filled with competitive blogs. Attracting viewers and increasing traffic to your site can be challenging ... but, it doesn't have to be. You can increase the traffic, plus, have many of these initial viewers coming back wanting to read more.

How to Strengthen Your Post – The Best Post

Amazing Content

- CHOOSE YOUR WORDS CAREFULLY – Supply high quality, applicable information.
- Give ... expecting nothing in return.
- Sprinkle facts and quotes from reputable resources.
- Have fun and let your true voice ring.

Impressive Presentation

- FIRST IMPRESSIONS COUNT – Be ready to change and "play" with the format.
- Write with a mixture of formality and conversational tones.
- Add an eye-catching picture.
- Vary the sentence format to include paragraphs, point form, and checklists.
- Emphasize important content using bold, caps, or underline.
- De-clutter and use spaces.

Cyberspace: The virtual world of computers and their networks—Internet, World Wide Web, or www.

Concise Format

- THE SHORTER THE BETTER—cut, cut, and then cut some more.

- Check adjectives and adverbs—"tiny" instead of "very small."

- Choose the strongest verb possible—"shuffled" or "sprinted" instead of "ran quickly."

- Write in active rather than passive voice—"Traffic drove to my site where my products were sold" instead of "Traffic was driven to my site where my books were sold."

- Use precise phrases instead of run-on sentences—"functioning links" instead of "links that connect one site to another site where the viewers will be led."

- Reread the article and tighten—"the reader's review" instead of "the review of the reader."

Expect revisions. Let the post simmer. Return, and make even more changes. To attract <u>massive exposure</u> and have these initial viewers coming back, write posts using **amazing content** with **impressive presentation** in **concise format**.

Massive Exposure: Appearance in many places, expanding your Network.

Jo-Anne's Top 5 Pieces of Advice for a Successful Blog

1. Be prepared to market and promote your blog.

2. Present your blog in a professional and user-friendly manner. It must be attractive for the viewer.

3. Target your audience. Submit relevant, factual, and interesting information where the reader can contribute.

4. Discover the balance between selling and presenting. Feel comfortable expressing yourself. Have fun ... it will show in your "voice."

5. Edit. Polish each post. Make sure you have included all widgets that are necessary for your viewer to navigate and gain the knowledge they seek.

Blogging

ADVANCING IN THE SEARCH ENGINES
(Search Engine Optimization – SEO)

Keywords and Phrases fuel the Search Engines

*W*hether you are building a retail platform or marketing your product(s), the main goal in creating a blog is to attract an audience and drive potential customers back to your site where the items are sold.

Producing an article with great content is a must. It's very competitive out there, and new <u>lurkers</u> rarely just stumble onto your blog. But there are some techniques that can put you into the drivers seat so you can *conquer all obstacles*.

You are the chauffeur. The noise behind you is becoming louder and louder. You peer over your shoulder, eyes wide, and the stretch limo you've been driving is bulging with customers. *But how did they get there*, you are wondering?

How do you add passengers to an empty vehicle?

Activate the web crawlers (<u>SEO</u>).

Use a catchy title that includes **keywords** and **key phrases**. Think outside the box. Get those creative juices flowing. When you create a snazzy title that includes keywords or key phrases, the hungry web crawlers are attracted to them as choice morsels.

Lurker: A person who reads blog discussions but never comments.

SEO: Search Engine Optimization. A strategy used to boost your site higher in the Search Engine Page Rank.

Repeat, repeat, repeat. Sprinkle the keywords and key phrases throughout the great content in your post without sounding robotic.

Choose your keywords and key phrases wisely.

- **Select keywords and key phrases** that your potential audience might use in their searches (Google/Yahoo/Bing, etc.). Put yourself in their shoes and ask: "What word(s) would I search to find what I'm looking for?"

- **Be specific.** Using the highest description, such as "author" or "plumbing" will make it very difficult for your potential buyer to find you. Instead, bring it closer to your specialty by using phrases like "inspirational author" or "home plumbing supplies." This helps narrow the search. I suggest using your name with your business. Now we're talking.

- **Fill in the tags.** Add these same keywords and key phrases as tags at the bottom of the post and again on the directed Social Bookmarks (Digg/Stumble/Delicious, etc.). (Note: Are you unfamiliar with a "tag" and what it does? Check out our **Glossary** at the end of this book.)

The search engine is the limo, and you're the driver. Never let your tank run dry. Fill it with the proper fuel. Add selective keywords and phrases into the tank. It will fuel your engine and take you far. As the limo driver, you have that control. You can *conquer all obstacles*.

Links – Functioning Blogs / Websites

Recently, I followed through with a friend's request. She wanted me to check her website and blog. Frustrated, she asked me if there was anything she could do. Apparently, she had posted great content but was puzzled when there had been no traffic. Her fabulous articles sat empty of recorded visitors. She wanted an interactive blog, a place to discuss her book with the audience. She was ready to give up, and stop writing.

Glancing through her site, I immediately noticed a very important missing component. She had nothing down the sides—no added widgets and, thus, no links.

Why add widgets?

The word "widget" probably evolved from the term "window gadget." It is usually an icon with embedded program code. It can be static, only containing an external link, or it may show some kind of changing information, such as the number of visitors to a site, a map of their locations, a mini-browser, or a simple "click here" to follow this blogger. Searching online for the word "widgets" will yield a plethora of these little mini-programs. Most of them give you HTML code that can be copied and pasted into a widget spot within your blog.

Adding widgets to your site, especially widgets with links, is an important way to attract web crawlers. Search engines have web crawlers "crawling" around the world wide web snagging new content and links. Like your great product that sits on the shelf unnoticed, your blog/ website will remain lonely and unvisited until you have something that draws attention to it—until you take action. It is imperative for the search engines to discover your blog.

Are there other ways to activate web crawlers?

Yes, there are other ways to activate web crawlers to snag onto your blog and boost it higher in the search engine <u>rankings</u>. Great content and high

---

Rank (Page or Search Engine): Indicates the page on which your link or site shows up in Search Results. The goal is to be on the first page.

traffic will draw attention, but there are other tactics that will ensure the recognition your site deserves. Wisely selecting the **keywords and phrases**, and repeating them often, will get you more attention. But there's more …

External Links

It is up to you to link your blog to high traffic sites and to maintain the links' functionality.

Your blog template probably contains a section below the "Widget" section on your sidebar called "Links." Links can be added under categories such as <u>Blogroll</u>, Favorites, Resources, etc. You can determine the title of each category and the number of high traffic blogs or sources you wish to include.

Note: **Proper ethics:** *Request permission from other bloggers prior to linking them to yours.*

Comments

Adding comments to high traffic sites will establish short duration links back to your site. Comment, comment, comment. This also lets bloggers know that their efforts are appreciated, or not!

Tips

- **Alexa.com** – Visit the Alexa.com site. Alexa has created a nifty toolbar you can upload onto your computer that displays a graph to monitor the actual traffic to the site you are investigating and considering for a link to your blog. Linking to a low traffic site is not profitable. Just watch the bar, and you will know if it's worth your time and trouble.

- **Mashable.com** – Mashable.com is a social media guide with very high traffic. By registering and adding content (a blog post), you can link this site back to your blog by listing it under the widget category "Resources." You have now targeted a different audience that will branch farther out into cyberspace and generate further buzz for you and your product(s).

- **Note:**
  1. Never leave your sidebar widgets empty of links.

Blogroll: A list of other blog sites that are recommended by the blogger, usually placed in the sidebar.

2. Change the term "category" to TITLES. It's more user friendly, and viewers will be able to identify with this "changed" term.
3. Check the links periodically to make sure they are still active. Links can be broken when addresses change. Make the best use of the space you have available by having working links.

Internal Links

- **Link your own sites together** – If you have more than one blog/ website, add the links to the sidebar widget of each one. I have three blogs:

  1. Premium Promotional Services – Complete Marketing Services
  2. Conquer All Obstacles – Marketing Tips for Writers
  3. Jo-Anne Vandermeulen – Journey to Publication

  I make sure I have listed each site on the sidebar of each of my sites. This links them all together. The traffic will flow from one to the other, and I don't have to do anything else.

- **Link your sites to your social media networks** (Facebook, MySpace, LinkedIn, Twitter, and Google+, etc.) **and back to your blog** – Using their fancy buttons or icons can replace the name and link itself, but check out the appearance of your blog after adding such buttons. Too many, too big, too flashy can distract your viewers from their main focus, which should be the article you have posted.

෴

After viewing my friend's site and showing her the importance of using widgets and links in those sidebars, she added her other sites and networks down the sides of both her website and blog. This served two purposes:

1. Her audience could now follow what interests her;
2. Traffic flowed properly allowing the web crawlers to do their job.

My friend is back to writing great content articles for her blog. She is receiving the traffic she had hoped for and is thrilled with the interaction she is having with her audience. She has even noticed an unbelievable hike in sales. Now a "happy camper," she has learned to *conquer all obstacles*.

Long-Tailed Keywords

*Y*ou can *conquer all obstacles* by carefully selecting the keywords to use in your title, throughout your content, and insert in the tag section. Your ultimate goal is to boost your site higher in the search engine rankings.

How do I optimize my search engine ranking?

Optimize your position in the major search engine rankings by:

- **Registering your site on the major search sites.**

    If you don't know how to do this, just Google "register my URL on search engines," and it will take you to the registration pages.

- **Supplying great content.**

    If you know what to say but are not sure of your writing skills, hire an <u>editor</u>. It will be worth it in the long run. (I recommend Nancy E. Williams – TheLaurusCompany.com. Nancy and her staff can "think outside the box.")

- **Selecting great <u>long-tailed keywords</u>.**

    Selecting great long-tailed keywords begins with your title. A catchy title will attract the readers, but it may remain invisible to the web crawlers. To make both happy, try mixing your titles. One day, think outside the box and supply a catchy title. For the next post, use a more descriptive or technical title. For example, the title of this section, "Long-Tailed Keywords," may sound interesting for someone searching for information on keywords, but those reading for entertainment may scan the title and pass it by. Our goal is to attract the web crawlers and boost our post high into the search engines to enable those searching for our information to find it.

    Even though my own site is registered with the search sites and my

---

Editor: The person who puts a literary work into acceptable form with accurate syntax, grammar, spelling, and punctuation. Also, one who manages the editorial process.

Long-Tailed Keywords: A combination of words making up a keyword phrase that helps narrow the selection category in a search engine.

content is relevant, my objectives are clearly defined in my titles. One of my favorite posts was called, "Turning Nightmares Into Pleasant Dreams." Although it was a catchy title for my followers, it would probably get missed by the web crawlers. A title such as "Links: Functioning Blogs/ Websites," however, will snag the web crawlers' attention and boost that article higher in the search engine rankings.

The World Wide Web contains massive amounts of information, and we are competing with hundreds of thousands of other similar topics. As business people, our ultimate goal is to be noticed by potential customers. When a potential customer types into the Google search bar what they are interested in purchasing, our name and product should be on the first few pages of their Search Results.

> *The purpose of using keywords and key phrases is to aid the search engines in matching information that is typed into a browser search bar with information in the search engine <u>databases</u>.*

How do I get on a potential customer's first page search results?

Carefully select the right **long-tailed keywords** for your title, and then repeat these long-tailed keywords several times in your post or site page. This will give you a boost higher in the search engines and drive massive traffic to your site.

Google Keyword Tool

Google has developed a tool that will aid you in creating good keywords for your site. When you enter your URL (the link to your site), the tool will scan your page and suggest relevant keywords. You can find this tool by searching for "Google Keyword Tool."

Carefully check out the charts. A keyword such as "marketing" will receive massive clicks, but it will be impossible to compete against all the other bloggers and webmasters who have also used "marketing" as their keyword.

If you use a string of words—a "long-tailed keyword"—along with "marketing," you will see the clicks are still massive, but suddenly you are

---

Database: A collection of related data organized for easy access, such as a collection of email addresses.

now a competitor in the race.

Using the Google Keyword Tool will help you *conquer all obstacles* and "win the race." Supplying the selected keywords in your title and throughout your post or page will attract the web crawlers' attention and boost your site higher in the search engine rankings.

It's time to get noticed and bring attention to yourself.

Climbing To the Top – A Search Engine Perspective

ou have learned how to be a Professional Blogger. Your Content is relevant, informative, and interesting, and you are logging more followers. Now, to *conquer all obstacles* and get your site climbing higher in those search engines, you must be prepared to do some work. Sure, establishing a readership so those hits multiply in numbers is important, but now you will have to convince the web crawlers.

How do I optimize my site in a search engine's perspective?

Register your site on the top three search engine sites: Google, Yahoo, and Bing. Those three will get the ball rolling. In case you are interested, the Approximate Market Share[†] of the search engines as of August 2011 is:

Google - Global	82.76%
Yahoo - Global	6.57%
Baidu	4.77%
Bing	3.76%
Ask - Global	0.55%
AOL - Global	0.39%
Excite - Global	0.02%
Lycos - Global	0.02%
Microsoft Live Search	0.00%
MSN - Global	0.00%
AltaVista - Global	0.00%

[†]http://marketshare.hitslink.com/search-engine-market-share.aspx?qprid=4

You can search the sites to find out how to register your site, but is really not necessary to register at all of them. Registering with the top three will cause the smaller search engines to hop on board. Google actually says it's not necessary to submit your site because they will find you! They find you primarily through links from other sites. However, if links from other sites are in short supply, be sure to submit your site. Once is enough. But please have your site finished and polished before doing so.

Climbing up the search engine rankings takes time. Results are not going to happen overnight.

> *"In my experience, it is not until a blog is 6 to 12 months old that it really begins to grow in its authority in Google."*
>
> —ProBlogger *"How to Grow Your Blog to the Next Level With SEO"*
> (SEO = Search Engine Optimization)

Also register your site with **Linkreferral.com** or **Socialize It**. Link these tag mechanisms by pasting their link on your page or site. For example, if you want your selling page to be the focus, make sure you place their symbol and links on that specific page. If you look on my Premium Promotional Services site, you will see the buttons placed in the widgets on the side bar and at the bottom of the main page. After the site is registered and you have linked sites, click on the buttons and tag your site using as many mechanisms as possible (ex: Digg, StumbleUpon, Bookmark, etc.). Don't forget to include the tags. Bold the keywords, and add them to heading tags and images.

Add more links. With your quality content, the traffic to your site will increase. Soon, others will make contact to link their blog with yours. Check out their site first. Go with your gut reactions. It doesn't hurt to reach out to others and request linkage, but you don't want to link to unsavory sites. By accumulating links in a similar niche, the keywords tagged will be emphasized and climbing the ladder in the ranking process will speed up.

Keep track of your stats. Analyze where the traffic is centralizing. Increase the internal links to these pages by adding extra links to the page. Include and highlight some of these pages in your sidebar or at the bottom of your posts. Again, don't forget to link the topic so your readers will simply navigate back to the high traffic topic. Don't delete these <u>pingbacks</u>; instead, highlight and apply them to your site. You may even decide to publish another post on the similar topic of interest.

You can *conquer all obstacles* by taking the time to manipulate the search engines to increase the ranking stats of your site. With more traffic heading to your site where your products or services are for sale, your odds for greater sales are increased.

Targeting Mountains Instead of Mole Hills

*I*magine seeing steep vertical slopes and sharp peaks. You welcome the sight, and it brings a smile to your face. Not often in life do we anticipate the mountains. Blowing things out of proportion is something we avoid. Wouldn't we rather face the mole hills? Not when we open our <u>Dashboard</u> and click on "stats."

Whether we are talking about our main site where the potential customer can purchase our products or services, or the blog we use to generate our following, the main goal is to keep those viewers coming back and increase our following.

So, how do we *conquer all obstacles* and get that line to keep climbing on the visual graph within our stats page?

Create Great Content

• Structure, facts, grammar, spelling, and punctuation do play an important role, but there is more. The content must have "feeling," an underlying logic and flow that is easy to absorb.

• The content must provoke an emotional response from readers and challenge them with a powerful call to action.

Dashboard: An interactive user interface that organizes and presents information in a way that is easy to read and manipulate. The skeleton of your blog—the place to design, add or move widgets, change settings and appearance, include media, and store stats.

Pingbacks: A notification that another blogger on the Internet linked to one of your posts in their post. It shows up as a comment in your post and includes a link back to their post where you can approve, delete, or spam the pingback.

• Discover that balance between challenging the reader to understand your message, creating the truth, and producing facts without coming across as "dry." Produce content that is interesting, challenging, and informative, something the reader can take away in awe or with a "wow." Don't hide important information, thoughts, or steps, but don't toss it in their lap either. Reread your post before publishing, and omit unnecessary words. Try it, and be amazed at the results.

• The most important thing in content marketing is reliability. You must produce consistently or the readers just won't show up, and the mole hill will prevail. The plan is simple. Schedule your posts, be genuine to your followers, and get the content out the day you promised.

Simple Strategies That Will Generate New Readers and Keep Your Original Readers Coming Back

• **Remind the reader to subscribe.** Remember, there are newbies coming to your site all the time. Sure, you posted the directions initially, but it doesn't hurt to post the simple instructions again. I do this at the bottom of the odd posts:

> *Interested in having Jo-Anne Vandermeulen's "Conquer All Obstacles" bi-weekly posts automatically deposited in your email? Please subscribe for FREE by clicking on the button on the side widget of this blog.*

• **Send or post an invitation to subscribe and to invite a friend.** Viral promotion generates readers.

> *"If you receive this email from a friend, click here for a free subscription to [Your Blog Name] (link your site). Got a friend that could do with some tips on marketing and promotion? Let them know about [Your Blog Name] by forwarding this email on to them."*

All of this sounds incredibly easy, but it works. My stats looked more like mountains than mole hills. You can *conquer all obstacles* by using these tactics in your next post. So simple.

Blogging

JO-ANNE'S FAVORITE TIPS

Perfecting Your Blogging Skills

*Y*ou have decided to blog. Wonderful! After a few posts, sit back, and think about these questions and answers:

1. ***Why am I blogging?***
    To create a platform.

2. ***What am I hoping to gain from blogging?***
    Followers (potential buyers) who will revisit my site.

3. ***Who am I targeting for a viewing audience?***
    People who are interested in my product(s).

Let's assume blogging is a learned skill.

Seven Steps to Help Perfect Your Blogging Skills

1. ***How's that title working for you?***
    A headline has less than a second of a site visitor's attention, so it had better be compelling. The title must catch the viewer's attention and draw them into the rest of your post. Is your title short, worded to benefit the reader?

2. ***Include a picture.***
    Images will hold the viewer a tad longer than a page filled with straight information.

3. ***Break up the information.***

Include subtitles or highlighted bold keywords that help the viewer scan to see if they want to stop and absorb. Again, KISS—Keep It Simple, Sweetie! Simple is better.

4. ***Let your voice ring true.***

Show yourself—that you're human. Conversational or informal language is more receptive and will hook your audience. Share experiences and interesting information to show credible authority; but also include the odd error or mistake you've made in the past. Can you open yourself to show vulnerability? Transparency works wonders—draws attention, gains trustworthiness, and gathers true friends. Don't forget to display a photo of yourself. Our brains are wired to create relationships with faces.

5. ***Chosen topic.***

To decide on the content for your article, research through past stats to check where your audience lingers the most, what topics have the greatest hits, and which posts gathered the highest number of comments. But don't let that stop you from taking a chance. Waiver from the usual by slipping in just one post and and see what happens. Adding flavor doesn't hurt. And you never know when another door may open.

6. ***Put your best stuff up top.***[†]

Did you know the top of the page gets about 17 times more exposure than the areas near the bottom? If 40% to 50% of the viewers leave your blog after the first page, put your best foot forward. Don't leave the best for last. Think of this as a sprint instead of a long distance race. Present the best information first and in a tight manner.

7. ***Presentation is everything.***

First impressions are lasting impressions. A site that is simple to navigate and read will attract viewers. I have discovered from reading through several subjective comments from site reviewers that most readers do not like music, flashy pictures, and wallpapered backgrounds. KISS is the key ingredient to an attractive site.

[†]Reference: Step #6 facts collected. "Absolute Scrolling Report" done by Clicktale Researchers. http://blog.clicktale.com/2007/12/04/clicktale-scrolling-research-report-v20-part-2-visitor-attention-and-web-page-exposure/

Again, ask yourself ... *What is the purpose of my blog?* If you have designed your blog to build an audience, you must serve the viewers. Now the blogging isn't about you; it's about them. It's time to read your next post content through their eyes.

Eight Tips to Successful Blogging

*D*o you *conquer all obstacles* by writing posts that attract readers and keep them coming back because they can relate to you?

1. **Write with honesty and authenticity.**

Admitting your character defects and insecurities when posting an article shows others that you are "human," no matter where you are in your successes.

One of my biggest fears in life is getting lost. Gosh, my palms get sweaty just thinking about it. Having no sense of direction is a daunting fear for many when it comes to marketing and causes a sense of being lost. But fear no more. I can guide you down a straight, clear path to promoting yourself and your products. To *conquer all obstacles* is to have direction.

> *All you have to do is devise a specific plan and discover your balance.*

2. **Write in conversational style, braiding in the formal style of facts.**

Read your post aloud. You can hear your words more clearly than keeping them in your head. Ask yourself if what you said would hold the attention of your readers. Vary your sentence length. This strengthens your writing and builds rhythm. A great title can capture the attention of your audience.

3. Write with emotion and feel the words you're sharing. Really express your passion.

Being positive and stating facts shows that you respect your passion and are nearly obsessed with sharing the news. Avoid the phrases, "I think," "maybe," and the direct phrase, "you should." Keep them out of your posts. Write with authority, but don't tell people what to do; let them make their own inferences. As bloggers, our job is not only to supply valuable content, but to make the reader feel special. I use the brand or motto, "*conquer all obstacles*," because it fits EVERYTHING I truly believe my audience can attain. You CAN *conquer all obstacles*.

4. Write with a blend of emotions—be funny, heart-warming, and motivating.

This is an area I have to work at and consciously apply. I can be motivating with no problem, but I often feel that I'm too serious. Here is one post I purposely added to remind myself: ***The last time you read something that made you laugh, did you walk away?***

One of the most responsive status updates on my Facebook home page was a one-liner, fill-in the blank: ***I know when I've been on the Internet too long when I_____.***

5. *Are you speaking from the heart?*

Do you show empathy? Open yourself to your audience by sharing honest examples of your own life. Show that you understand and care.

Write with no fear. This is no time to consider judgments from others. What we say is subjective. Our job is not to make everyone happy. Take chances and open yourself up. You will be amazed at how many others relate to your story and come on board, not just as followers, but as fans.

6. Make your post easy to read. Avoid run-on sentences and long paragraphs.

Objectively read what you have written. Will readers enjoy reading it? Is it clear and concise? Have you communicated what you wanted to say in a way that is easy to understand? Disjointed and confusing posts will drive people away. If you recognize that you have shortcomings in your writing, hire an editor. It will pay off in the long run. People will appreciate your professionalism.

7. **Take your time posting your article. Let it stew on the back burner for awhile.**

When I think of a topic for my blog post, I usually sleep on the title. Not literally—it's like after completing a manuscript. The idea or writing needs time to cool. In posting an attention grabbing article, the idea and especially the title needs time to simmer. And I happen to do my best thinking in REM.

8. **Always write what fascinates you.**

The writing should come easily as you enjoy the process. If not, it may be time to ask yourself about your niche or passion.

Successful Blogging = Engaging the Reader

Jo-Anne's Vital Blog Checklist

❑ An attractive image of your product is visible even before the reader scrolls.

❑ A tab indicates more information about the product(s) (brief synopsis, reviews, etc.)

❑ A purchase button is (preferably) embedded in the product image or directly under it.

❑ The link to the purchase button goes directly to the purchase page.

❑ A brief personal bio is available, including your full name.

❑ A tab or button is included where readers can connect directly with you.

❑ Your posts include valuable information for your audience and will be an awesome sample of your voice.

Are You Guilty of Copyright Infringement?

*A*re you aware that you may be breaking the law? If you are using images from Google Images or other resources for pasting into your blog posts, you may be infringing on a copyright, and that's against the law!

A better resource for finding free images is Flickr (.com). You can use many of the photos posted there for your website without infringing on any copyrights. Just be sure to check each photo you like to see if it is in the Public Domain and/or copyright free.

Go to: http://www.flickr.com/search/advanced/

Then go to **Flickr Advanced Search** AND CHECK OFF ALL THREE BOXES AT THE BOTTOM FOR THE ADVANCED SEARCH.

Another resource site is:

http://www.blogsessive.com/blogging-tips/free-images-for-blogs/

Stay on the right side of the law when using images made by others. Take the time to be sure you are not infringing on a copyright.

Note from Jo-Anne

Convert your web or blog page (HTML) into PDF format. No registration, and FREE. http://html-pdf-converter.com/

Jo-Anne's Favorite Sticky Note Motivators

Do you keep quotes stickied to your bathroom mirror? In front of your toilet? In your car? Some of you are chuckling and nodding your heads. I find it is good to plan ahead for those times when we are feeling down and need a little motivation. The positive messages scrawled on my sticky notes give me what I can't find within. There are millions of inspirational slogans we can use to pull us up from a dark hole. Here are some of my favorites:

"When one door closes, another one opens."

"Keep your eyes open for the unexpected. Don't be afraid. Seize the opportunities before you."

"You have your own answers within you."

"Everybody is talented, original, and has something important to say."
—Brenda Ueland

"Imagination is the Divine Body in every Man." —William Blake

....

Sometimes, it is great just to know we are not alone. We all have a bad day every now and then. Have you ever caught yourself staring at an empty screen with a completely blank mind? If the creativity isn't there, here are a couple of suggestions from some famous people:

"Moving around is good for creativity: the next line of dialogue that you desperately need may well be waiting in the back of the refrigerator or half a mile along your favorite walk."
—Will Shetterly

"Writing ... is the closest men ever come to childbearing."
—Norman Mailer

Social Networking

GUARANTEEING MASSIVE EXPOSURE

Building Relationships Increases Readership

*f*or a business person, building a great platform worked last year, but if you are to remain competitive and in the forefront this year and the next, it will require more than a great platform.

Don't let this scare you away. I am going to give you some tips to help grow your presence on the Internet and guarantee massive exposure.

The Key to Successful Marketing is to Expand Your Network!

The major building block to forming relationships is our natural, built-in ability to converse. A successful networker will have to be CONNECTED. Having friends and building relationships has never been so important. Now is the time to chain to your follows and build a trusting bond.

How do we make friends and build relationships?

1. **Accept Invitations**
   a. Post memorable comments
   b. Guest post
   c. Participate in interviews
   d. Conduct interviews by asking intelligent questions and responding graciously

2. **Attend Conferences and Workshops**
   a. Contribute to chat discussions
   b. Whisper answers to individual participants
   c. Give positive encouragement

> *Be positive and energetic.*
> *Your enthusiasm will be felt through the net-waves.*

3. **Spark Interactions by Networking on Social Media Sites**
   a. Ask an irresistible question
   b. Generate a discussion that others will view with interest
   c. Keep the discussion active by inviting lurkers to contribute
   d. Show that ALL folks are important regardless of who they are

4. **Join Private Groups Based Around Your Niche**
   a. Supply clear and concise answers to any questions
   b. Back your answers with credentials with prior written posts or quotes
   c. If you don't have the answer, steer them in the right direction
   d. Keep a balance between conversational writing style and formality

> *Showing that you are knowledgeable and approachable*
> *makes you very attractive.*

5. **Reciprocity**
   Supply others with what they want.

6. **Provide a Link Back to Your Site Where Your Products Are Sold**
   In all correspondence (email, group chat, conferences, guest posts, etc.), leave your <u>signature</u> with a link back to your site/profile.

With time and persistence, lurkers will become followers, and followers will become fans. Take the time and make the effort to create lasting relationships.

Signature: Up to 4 lines stating the name, label of expertise, product name, and site address. Commonly used at the bottom of email messages. Not the same as a digital signature that is encrypted to provide verifiable proof of authorship.

The best gift you can give is your time.

Show your appreciation. It goes a long way. Friends bring along more readers. They will take you under their wing and introduce you to other popular networkers who have their own following. Accept connections by linking their blog to yours and vise versa. Continue doing favors, expanding your network, and producing great content in your blog. You will soon see great results.

Social Networking Equals Success

*O*ften during an interview, I am asked, "What's next for Jo-Anne Vandermeulen?" Believe it or not, what happens tomorrow is usually not planned nor in my control. I merely walk down the clear path, step forward and through the wide opening, and welcome the new and totally exciting experiences. Read on to see what I mean.

All in a Day's Work

Yesterday, two new doors opened, and I walked through …

First, while social networking, I met a newly published author from Australia. We agreed to trade guest blogging, and I had her as a special guest on my blog, Conquer All Obstacles. She was also a featured guest on "Authors Articulating with Jo-Anne Vandermeulen" on BTR (BlogTalkRadio). She returned the favor by publishing an article in her blog. Her blog has a circulation of around seven million people combined. Four million of those people are in Sydney. Talk about MASSIVE EXPOSURE! And to a part of the world that would have been near impossible to reach a decade ago.

Did this form of marketing cost me lots of money? No! Absolutely nothing. Social networking is free. All you have to do is be proactive. Roam the World Wide Web and meet others, form relationships, and promote each other.

The second door opened, and again, I walked through …

As I have reached out to other hosts on BTR, I have been privileged to be a special guest on various shows. Yesterday, a featured BTR program called "The Publishing Insiders" had me as their special guest. All I had to do was reach out and ask. As a team, we produced an amazing one-hour show called "Amp Up Your Online Book Promotion" (my genre).

I then discovered that "The Cyrus Webb," a show on which I was featured, was not only syndicated through the Internet, but also through many U.S. FM radio stations.

It's all about EXPOSURE, and opportunities are out there. Social networking equals success. All we have to do is take the steps and reap the rewards. Never have we been in such an amazing position to build our business platforms, create massive exposure, and sell our products.

Massive Exposure With www Promotion

I am convinced that positive energy travels through cyberspace. Massive exposure comes from networking. Social networking equals success. Massive exposure comes with World Wide Web promotion.

How to Create Massive Exposure

1. **Expect nothing in return**.
   Completely unconditional.

2. **Be genuine**.
   Hidden or twisted motivation will sift through your voice. If you have an attitude of giving, you will create massive exposure for you and the products you sell.

3. **Be vulnerable**.
   If you are open and true to your audience, you will attract followers who will become your fans, fans who will trust and soon purchase your products.

My own success is proof that it can be done. At 15 months, I was responding to over 50,000 followers with an audience of over 11 million people! Positive energy does travels through cyberspace. Massive exposure comes from networking, teaming together, and unconditionally giving all you have to offer. If I can *conquer all obstacles*, so can YOU!

Marketing – Using Social Media

*H*ow will you perceive the social media? If you are new to blogging and involving yourself in the social media sites like Facebook, Google+, and Twitter, you do have a choice on how to handle this new form, or tool, of marketing. Your choice breaks down to your reactions to technology. You can either run away in fear, pretend it doesn't exist, or just grab the bull by the horns and hold on tight.

You can jump on this new fast craft and *conquer all obstacles*. All it takes is a change of attitude. Perception is HUGE. Isn't it time to see the glass as half full rather than half empty?

> **Make this the year of opportunity, a year to begin successfully using the social media revolution to your advantage.**

You're a newbie? Don't worry. We were all exactly where you are today at one point. We can relate. We remember what it was like to start our first blog, to make our first 140-character Twitter announcement, and to create our first profile on Facebook.

Like writing, begin with the rough draft. Don't worry about your punctuation. If you forget to fill out all the blanks in your social media profile or half of your message gets cut off when twittering, there are reminders and second chances. Your second draft will be a lot better than the first. Whenever I'm scared, I ask myself: *What's the worst thing that can happen?* and *Is it life-threatening?*

Jump in and do it. Open up that first social media network and fill out your profile. Don't know something? Heck, don't worry about it. You can always Google your question. And there are plenty of people within the social media community who are willing to help those who appear stranded. Reach out and click the mouse that hovers over a member and request a friendship. Just reading that person's profile has sparked some sort of interest your way. And that's it! You've begun your journey into marketing using the social media.

A positive attitude goes a long way. It will show in your voice, the articles you write, and even in the short bursts of communication on Twitter. Staying positive is one of the secrets in attracting potential customers.

Why Start A Blog

A blog establishes your authority. It says you are an expert on a particular subject. A blog is your home base and will become your identity and place of presence.

Writing posts about your passion will be easy once you have faced your fear. If you're struggling or dreading this task, chances are you haven't discovered your true niche. It may be time to switch gears and take a self-inventory, asking yourself what you love doing the most.

How do I Create Quality Posts or Valuable Content?

• **Create articles around topics of your passion.** Sell each post within the first paragraph. Like your story, it's imperative to hook the reader from the first sentence or paragraph.

• **Stay positive, and maintain a balance** between using informative and conversational language styles.

• **Produce posts containing intelligent, useful, and newsworthy content.**

• **Promote others** using quotes with direct reference (if you can, use links). Others will appreciate the "mentions" and your post will become stronger with the proven, backed-up facts.

• **Ask for help** when you need it. Again, a win-win situation.

• **Spend extra time researching and educating yourself.** Read, read, and let me say it again … read!

- **Become a two-way blogger.** View and comment on other blogs. The blogger will appreciate your following, and other lurkers will read your response, become curious, and may direct themselves back to your profile where your blog link is located.

Soon after you push that publish button, some of your viewers will respond to your post, and positive interaction has begun. (Remember there will be many, many lurkers—viewers who will read your post but will not respond right away—but they are out there, watching, reading everything you write). Your viewers will begin to share your name and quality content with others. Bingo! You have now graduated into the current of social media—marketing you and your products and services.

Turning Nightmares Into Pleasant Dreams

*I*magine yourself on a dark stage, in the largest theater hall in the world. Everything is quiet. The curtain lifts. Suddenly, the light is blinding. Before your eyes, over a billion people are cheering in the crowd. They are waving money in the air, chanting for you to speak about your products or services.

What if I told you this isn't a dream? You are on stage. There are two billion customers out there waiting and wanting to find you.

> **FACT**: *The number of Internet users worldwide has reached the two billion mark, according to the head of the UN's telecommunications agency, Hamadoun Toure.[†]*

Even though we are living in tough economic times, people are still spending money. Your customers are waving money, wanting to purchase your goods.

[†] Source: PhysOrg.com – Jan. 26, 2011. www.physorg.com/news/2011-01-internet-users-worldwide-billion.html

FACT: *The U.S. Census Bureau News reported June 2011 advance estimates of U.S. retail and food services sales of $387.8 billion, an increase of 8.1% above the previous year.*[†]

Right now, there's a problem. Your potential customers can't find you. They don't even know you exist. Suddenly, this wonderful dream has turned into a nightmare. The curtain lifts, and you are looking out into a theater hall that is empty. All is quiet, and you are alone.

When your curtain lifts, what do you see? Are you living a dream come true, or are you tossing and turning as the nightmare continues?

Many good businesses go unnoticed. Many great products sit on the shelves, never to be sold.

So how do you navigate the Internet to get two billion users to witness your outstanding performance and products?

Answer: Through promotional tactics, proper website fundamentals, strategies, techniques, and reading many resources as to how to market and sell your product(s) through the Internet.

The keys to success when it comes to marketing your product online:

- Target your audience
- Create a buzz
- Drive traffic
- Create a presence
- Provide proof that your product is a must-have

If you have the time, energy, and knowledge, you can make the profits you deserve. Rest assured, you can have pleasant dreams and wake-up with a smile on your face every day.

[†] Source: www.census.gov/retail/

Target Your Audience: Focus your energy toward viewers who may be interested in your product (gathering a following).

Monitor Web Activity with Alerts

*N*ow you get to be a fly on the wall. Who's wall? Everyone's wall who is talking about you. How? Sign up for the two <u>Alerts</u> listed below, and fill in the keywords (names or sites) you wish to be alerted about. You will then be alerted automatically via email whenever those keywords are mentioned or have activity. This is a great way to find out when someone is talking about you or your business.

Google Alerts – http://www.google.com/alerts
Twitter Alerts – http://tweetbeep.com/

Why is this important?

This information will tell you if your webcrawlers are working and if you have chosen wise tags (keywords). If the alerts are sending you your own pages that you have social bookmarked (added to Delicious, Digg, Bookmarks, StumbleUpon, etc.), it means you are doing a great job with your internal links.

When I have been a guest blogger on other sites, the alerts have sent me the name of the site with my name quoted. I can then send this information back to the presenter and let them know that their internal links are active. Chances are, they are ranking high in the search engines. (The higher your ranking in the search engines, the greater the chances are that your potential customers are going to find you and your business.)

Alerts has also caught others using my personal quotes as their own. Whether it's stealing or infringement on copyrights, it is wrong. If you are going to use material from others, give them proper reference. GRRrrrrr!

> *Use Alerts to prove the effectiveness of your promotional and marketing techniques.*

Alerts (Google): A service offered by Google, the search engine company, that notifies users when content from news, web, blogs, videos, or other groups matches search terms that have been pre-selected by the user in the Google Alerts service.

I use Alerts to prove the effectiveness of my promotional and marketing techniques. When I'm promoting, my plan is to create massive exposure. Every day I expect Alerts to pick up "Jo-Anne Vandermeulen," "Conquer All Obstacles," and "Premium Promotional Services." If I don't see the Alerts picking up my tags, then I know I'm not doing my job or there is a problem. I need to reactivate my internal links and social bookmark my pages. This is why linking blogs with other active bloggers is a great idea. When they social bookmark their page, your tags will automatically be marked and sent to Alerts. A double win.

Creating a Platform

ATTRACTING CLIENTS

A Perfect Pitch - A Sure Win!

Short, sweet, with an amazing hook ... and I'm not talking about a curve ball. To *conquer all obstacles* you must create a platform that stands out from the rest, and you must learn how to "pitch."

At first, creating a pitch will feel awkward. Writing a page, condensing it to a paragraph, and finally, to a sentence all takes cognitive thinking. Yet, you can feed off of this process and soon turn it into a cheering victory! Attitude is the answer. Creating a pitch is NOT grueling work. It is a challenge, a win with even more opportunities, and the reward is worth the effort!

As marketers, the competition is fierce. We need to stand out from the rest and prove we are the best.

As bloggers, we need to create valuable content in a short article that will leave the reader enriched and have them coming back for more.

Elevator pitch: A 30 to 60 second opportunity to make a powerful first impression and hook a prospect.

Most of us have heard the term "elevator pitch." It's a 30 to 60 second description of your business or product and why someone needs it. You have only 30 to 60 seconds to make a powerful first impression and hook your prospect before the elevator reaches the top and they are forever lost.

Presenting a pitch may be done in written form or verbal conversation. Some may be planned, but many of them will be unexpected "moments" when chatting with a stranger, an acquaintance, or a dear friend.

Creating a pitch is difficult, perhaps even more work than writing the article. A lot is on the line. Your audience, followers, fans, and even the door to your next opportunity may be at stake.

Prepare Your Pitch

Be Ready – Always be aware of these prime-time opportunities. Blend your pitch into conversation when the subject becomes available. As a teacher, we call these unexpected opportunities "teachable moments."

Have Your Pitch Polished and Rehearsed – Often your pitch will not be planned—a huge reason to have it rehearsed and polished. Observe your viewer. How's the eye contact? Are you keeping them interested?

Know When You've Said Enough – Again, through observation, you must read their body language. Usually, you will have less than a minute. Be ready to add your own "stories" or examples to hold their interest. But, fear no more. Simply:

1. **Begin with Action** – Leave out the "fluff" or back story.

2. **Revise** – Cut, cut, and cut some more. Take the time to rehearse verbally.

3. **Think** – Use astonishing words that attract, hook, and even shock the reader.

Now here's the good news...

Creating A Perfect Pitch Becomes Easier With Practice

Over time and with more experience, your pitches will become comfortable and automatic. No work at all! You will receive unbelievable rewards as the new opportunities begin to take over.

No matter if you're an author, blogger, or marketer, your record for wins will remain in tact. To throw a perfect game and *conquer all obstacles* is to perfect your pitch.

Building A Platform

*Y*ou must present a strong platform to get the attention of those coveted prospects. They want to read who you are, where you are established in the business world, and what you have to offer. So how do we make that happen?

One way is to hire a promoter to do it for you. If that's not in the budget or you feel confident you can do your own promotion, you have to provide a strong platform stating evidence of past successes and happy customers. This may be enough for those prospects to request more information.

I want to share with you my recent experience: I decided to submit one of my blog posts to Ezine Articles. No, I wasn't looking for cash payment. I was looking to build credits, to raise my platform as an author.

To my surprise, my article, "Turning Nightmares Into Pleasant Dreams," was immediately accepted and published.

I also earned Expert Author status. Well, now, doesn't that title sound pretty impressive in blog credits?

As an added bonus, I had been given notice that this article would appear on their high-traffic home page. Exposure!

Building a platform is similar to keeping past positive references from previous employees. It is a simple and painless way to build credits and show the experts just exactly who you are ... a fabulous business person with a fabulous product(s).

Audio Podcast – Promoting Through BlogTalkRadio

*R*eady to increase traffic back to your site? Don't let your profile and your goods just sit there. Promote through BlogTalkRadio.

Let's stir-up those webcrawlers; they love to snag variety forms of media. This will boost your name even higher in the search engines (Google, Yahoo, Bing).

By hosting your own show through BlogTalkRadio, you can create **FREE radio podcasts and syndicate your show to thousands of listeners** via Facebook, Twitter, MySpace, etc. By saving the link to your show(s) in your blog widgets, your followers and visitors can now simply click and listen right from your site.

Have you been asked to be a guest on someone else's show?

Go for it! Agreeing to be interviewed on a show will create a buzz that will generate massive exposure for you and your product(s).

Promoting the show through your site and syndicating the broadcast throughout social media networks will increase traffic back to your site. Talk about FREE promotion!

You can *conquer all obstacles* by going to www.blogtalkradio.com. Get a free registration, and begin your new journey.

It's simple. You only need a computer with an Internet connection and a telephone to host your own show and interact with your guests, or to be interviewed by other hosts.

All you have to do is:

1. **Register**

2. **Download iTunes** (to save shows) from www.apple.com/itunes/

Are you researching new material for your posts?

Through BlogTalkRadio, you can listen to personal encounters of original shows within your subject of interest. By downloading a show, you can then listen at a time that best suits you.

Perhaps you are searching for new material and want to listen to an interview relating to your subject. BlogTalkRadio allows participants to listen to original shows and even participate through computer chat or call-in when listening to the "live" program. You can ask the questions that are most pertinent to you.

You can *conquer all obstacles* by taking this step. Register for BlogTalkRadio, and roam the site. Click on all the tabs. Check out the **BlogTalkRadio Learning Center**, and hone in on the FAQs.

Start today. You have nothing to lose and everything to gain.

Twusted Twitter Twools and Twips

*W*hy is everyone talking about Twitter? Is this just a phase, or will this be the next form of interaction to replace our blogs?

Today, many social media networkers are twalking or twyping with what sounds like a "speech impediment." This is no speech impediment, however. This is the new world of Twitter.

Twitter

Twitter is a popular FREE micro-social network, a service enabling you to communicate and stay connected with others through the exchange of quick messages no longer than 140 characters. http://www.twitter.com

Twusted Twitter Tools

Today, there are many tools for Twitter users, and there are more and more surfacing all the time. Which tools will prove valuable to us depends on our needs and purposes for <u>tweeting</u>.

Just like blogging, if you want to *conquer all obstacles*, you must ask yourself, "Why am I tweeting?" If you are trying to build a platform, target an audience, and generate traffic back to your site where your goods are sold, then here are a few tools you cannot afford to be without:

- Twaitter – The Twaitter tool enables you to schedule recurring tweets. Free. http://www.twaitter.com/

- Tweetbeep – Discover what others are tweeting about that has to do with you. Twitter Alerts – http://tweetbeep.com/

- <u>**Bit.ly**</u> – Shorten, share, and track links (URLs). Reduces the URL length and makes sharing easier. http://bit.ly/pages/about/

Bit.ly: A utility that allows users to shorten the length of a URL and then track the resulting usage.

Tweet: A maximum 140-character post or status update on Twitter. Precise presentation packed with information. Note: Always include the link. Again, this will drive traffic to you and your product(s). Here's a recent example of a Tweet: #business #authors #blogtalkradio with @conquerall MARK YOUR CALENDARS! 24/10/2011 21:00 "INTERNET MARKETING MADE EASY"!

Twitter Tips

1. **Bio** – Look at your Twitter profile page. Most followers will read the one-line bio under "SETTINGS." Create a direct link to a profile page, rather than sending them to the homepage profile.

   Example: View the profile of JoVan@Prempromotions, Internet Promo Manager. http://bit.ly/2UV7y

2. **Follow-up** – Investigate your followers. Send them a direct message.

   Example: TY for following. I'm a BC gal, run my own Internet Promo business at: http://bit.ly/6aCh3 & Personal Blog at: http://bit.ly/pGGZX

3. **Feeds** – A simple feed that allows your Twitter post to automatically show up on your blog or website. Click on "SETTINGS," scroll down to "MORE INFO," and click on the blue link, "YOU CAN ALSO ADD TWITTER TO YOUR SITE HERE." Just follow the steps.

4. **Tweetdeck** – Syndicates the 140-character message automatically into status updates in Facebook, LinkedIn, and MySpace. Also categorizes incoming tweets so you can catch the ones that pertain to you. (Note: Hashtags # is a form of categorizing. If you see hashtags like "#Business" or "#mktg," then this tweet is for the attention of business people and marketers. If there is a topic of interest, perhaps where your audience would go, you can create a search column using the related hashtags, catching and managing your tweets that way, too.

5. **Promote** – Advertise your Twitter name or identity all over. Include your Twitter link in your signature. Add comments on Twitter discussions. Leave a direct message to others who are following you.

Take heed to the tools, sites, and tips shown here. When you begin to add a "w" after all of your "Ts," you know you've been tweeting a tad too long.

Add me on Twitter: http://www.twitter.com/conquerall

Hashtags: Indicated by the # symbol followed by a keyword or topic that categorizes messages. For example: If I'm tweeting about Internet Marketing, I would add the following hashtags: #mktg, #business, #authors.

Twitter Name: Indicated by the @ symbol followed by a username that identifies you. This will help lurkers to use your tweet name and direct others back to your twitter profile. For example: My twitter name is @conquerall.

Who Likes To Get Naked?

*G*OTCHA! A great title can capture the attention of an audience. And now that I have your attention, let's look at PLATFORMS—the reason why every business person should spend the time designing a bragging article about who you are and what you represent.

In a store or on the selling page of a site, your product(s) sits among thousands of others. Your blog or website hovers in cyberspace, naked, among millions of others.

Unless effectively promoted, it will sit shivering and all alone. You and your goods will blend in with the other business people and entrepreneurs like a chameleon taking on the appearance of its background.

Solution: You need to put some clothes on. And I mean dress up really well. You need to stop hiding from all the viewers and come forth. Building an impressive platform is the solution.

A platform is more than a bio. Just as a real platform elevates a speaker above his audience, you must discover ways to make yourself and your product(s) stand out from the crowd. Present yourself as Cinderella in the eyes of the Prince. Your platform must stand out from all the others.

This is not the time to be humble. You must really look at yourself in comparison to the others in your line of business and discover what makes you unique. Cinderella presented herself in a beautiful gown. Her beauty stood out from the crowd of possible prospects for the Prince. For you as a business, what descriptors hook the viewers' attention? Use both your character and your process of writing. Expose who you are and your voice. Really look at your work. What are your strengths? What captures your audience and keeps them wanting more? Be creative in your response. Show your voice in the explanation.

> *To *conquer all obstacles* you have to sell yourself.*

It's time to strip off your play clothes and squeeze into a business outfit. I know it doesn't feel comfortable, but it's necessary to attract viewers. This is not the time to blend into the crowd. Your platform matters.

Targeting Your Audience

SAVING ENERGY

Identify Your Audience

ou have built your platform and added to it as you have gained experience. Finally, you have ripped open the cardboard box and grabbed hold of your baby (okay, your product that you want to sell) and sucked in the wonderful aroma of success. With heart beating rapidly, it feels as if you could float up to the ceiling.

After you exhale and your eyelids flutter open, your next thought is:

"Where am I going to sell this, and who is going to buy it?"

You need an audience.

Ask yourself these questions:

1. *Who would be interested in my product(s)?*
Age, interest, sex, graphic location, intellectual ability, etc. Don't overwhelm yourself. Start with a character sketch and simply fill in the blanks. Visualize a viewer using your product, and go from there.

2. *Where would these people hang out?*
On the Internet, you have to know where to go virtually. There is no reason to waste your time barking up an empty tree. No use entering a room full of cat lovers to promote your dog. To *conquer all obstacles* is to really know your audience and to spend time in the social media sites where they are located.

Discover YOUR community, target this audience, and present your awesome platform. These viewers will VERY soon turn into your fans.

Twitter and Facebook – Sharing the Great News

*E*very now and then, I come across social media sites with amazing status updates that I can immediately apply. I love that! Two of my favorites are:

1. **Twellow – Twitter's Yellow Pages.** A fabulous strategy to target your audience and increase exposure for yourself. It is very simple to implement and has increased my followers tremendously. It's user-friendly and free! www.twellow.com

   a. Register for free.
   b. Find your targeting audience (category) and add yourself.
   c. Check out the sub-categories and add yourself there, too.
   d. Follow those you think will be interested in you.

2. **Facebook Business Pages**

   Why have a Facebook Business Page?

   a. The Facebook Business Page can accommodate a much larger audience, unlike the Facebook Profile page that has a 5,000 friend limit.
   b. All who "LIKE" your Facebook Business Page will receive the scrolling ticker on their Home Facebook Page.

   - Please feel free to browse, interact, and click the "Like" button on my Business Pages:

     1. Jo-Anne Vandermeulen – Romantic Fiction Author – "Conquer All Obstacles": http://on.fb.me/q3Hxs3

     2. Fans of Jo-Anne Vandermeulen – Group Page: http://on.fb.me/oHln9U

     3. Premium Promotional Tips for Writers: http://on.fb.me/pPEiEW

     4. Internet Marketing Made Easy: http://on.fb.me/n0DkZZ

How to Stand Out from the Rest

ow can you and your products stand out from the rest?

Attract An Audience

No one is going to know about your goods if you hide them among all the other goods in a store or cyberspace. Marketing your products and promoting yourself is a must.

How do we attract an audience with so much competition?

Meet The Needs Of Your Viewers

Times are changing. Flexibility is the answer in the business world. What worked yesterday may not work today. Think of targeting the market. Needs and interests are turning around. Promotion is never stagnant and neither is your message. Set aside some time to:

1. **Hook your audience** by frequently revisiting the brands and messages used.
2. **Analyze your successes** and build on your strengths, as well as improving your weaknesses.
3. **Make necessary changes** to enhance marketing tactics that work well with potential customers.

Marketing Message

Your marketing message is similar to a platform. The message you post must persuade viewers that you and your products stand higher than the rest. Your product is unique and the best on the market. This will generate more traffic to you and convince potential customers to buy your goods.

Take a good look at your message. Does it give the viewers what they are searching for? Are you in sync with your audience? This may take further research. Yes, this is time consuming but absolutely necessary. There is no use speaking out into an empty auditorium. Perhaps there is a generation gap. You may need to modernize your content so your followers can relate. YOU must be flexible and tap into their needs.

Discover Your Target Audience

It is your responsibility to get to know your audience by filling in the blanks and accumulating a specific description. Areas to look at might include:

- Genre
- Age
- Ethnic Background
- Classification (student, working, retired, etc)
- Interests, Hobbies and Lifestyle
- Perspectives, Attitudes and Values

Ten Ways to Convert Streams to Flowing Traffic

How would you like to turn a few viewers into thousands of followers? With flowing traffic comes a greater chance to sell your product(s).

To *conquer all obstacles* and draw potential clients to your products presented on the Internet, you must:

- **Be proactive.**
- **Make a constant effort.**
- **Reach your audience by getting out there.**
- **Have patience; it will take time.**
- **Be ready to roll-up your sleeves and persevere.**

I guarantee that all your hard work will pay off. The rewards are priceless. With flowing traffic heading back to your site, your product(s) will gain attention.

10 Ways to Draw Viewers to Your Site Where Your Products Are Sold

1. **Produce amazing comment replies** – Visit other blogs in your niche or area of expertise and leave well written comments that contain valuable content. Leave your signature. Follow the discussion.

2. **Providing a solution goes a long way** – Get out to other social media sites and prove you're an expert. Scan the discussions for questions

you can answer simply. Contribute by sharing similar experiences and empathize with the participants.

3. **Publicize your articles** – Gain "Expert Status" by submitting excellent articles from your blog. Ezine.com is one of many examples of recognized published postings (article directory) that not only attracts viewers, but is also another method to get your name and niche out there.

4. **Guest post or contribute articles on other blogs** – Each stream comes with its own readers. Many streams turn into a flow of traffic back to your site.

5. **Build your list of followers** – Reach out into various social media networks and gather friends. Interact to form trusting relationships.

6. **In your blog, vary the source of your posts by incorporating audio and visual podcasts** – Presentation is everything. Create catchy titles with appealing photographs. Supply the captions and posts with links back to your site. Include long-tailed tags/keywords. Submit videos and archived podcasts from BlogTalkRadio. Adding a presentation and interview also works well.

7. **Target the four largest media sites** – Facebook, Twitter, Google+, and LinkedIn are the growing fads today. Leave your signature with your site link. Update your profile within the media sites. Interested participants will want to know more about you, so make your site accessible through simple navigation.

8. **Educate your followers** – Provide simple guidelines or reminders. Encourage your followers to subscribe and tell them exactly how. Request your followers to promote you to others (their friends) with "Spread the word" or "Tell a friend".

9. **Find new potential followers** – Vary your targeting audience; don't always pitch to the same viewers. Know who you want to attract, and explore new ways to find them. Choose sites with major traffic, and take note of the secondary sites they are linked to.

10. **Activate the webcrawlers, and social bookmark each post** – Register your blog in Google, Yahoo, and Bing. After each post, ping the article (Digg, Delicious, Stumbleupon, etc.). SEO – Optimize your ranking in the search engines so your potential viewers can find you.

With flowing traffic comes a greater chance to sell your product(s).

Balancing Online Activities

MANAGING TIME

Social Media – Managing Your Time

If you are new to blogging, Twitter, Facebook, LinkedIn, Google+, etc., the constant changing and high speed of these social media sites can make a person feel overwhelmed. When bombarded with all of the social media sites, how often does the little voice in your head scream this fearful reality: "THERE'S NOT ENOUGH TIME!"

You can *conquer all obstacles* and stifle this fear by learning how to manage your time with project management.

According to Wikipedia[†], "project management" is *the discipline of planning, organizing, and managing resources to bring about the successful completion of specific project goals and objectives.*

Managing Time through Planned Media Activities

- **Chunk The Work**

Break down what needs to be accomplished into digestible morsels. Swallowing too much at one time will choke you, stop you in your tracks. Instead of setting a goal to send so many tweets a day or writing in your blog every day, break it down and simplify to suit your lifestyle.

- **Establish A Routine**

Plan the time of the day that works best for you. You may want to choose a time of day when you will be uninterrupted or when you are most rested. You will then be productive and work more efficiently. After a few weeks, assess your plan. Is the time of day working? Is the allotted time too long or too short? Once you feel relaxed, satisfied (not overwhelmed) and productive, begin planning weekly and then monthly media activities using this daily routine.

Now, stick with this schedule. Go ahead and mark it in your calendar, tell a friend or your family. A successful plan requires commitment, consistency, and monitoring your actions.

The following sample schedule works well for me in managing social network sites and activities:

DAILY

At least once daily (for me, first thing in the morning), takes about an hour:

- Check and respond to emails. Sort, organize, and file most.
- Produce or re-use a prior post in my blog.
- Respond to blog and group comments.
- Announce this post in Twitter, Facebook, LinkedIn, MySpace, and Google+ status using my twitter name, title, or what it is about, and the link.
- Create six to ten new tweet messages.
- Check Facebook profile, group, business pages, and respond where appropriate. Sort and add new friends, around 20 per day.
- Periodically and throughout the day, I set aside short time slots to tweet, blast retweets, and respond to emails (already developed from my hour planned routine). Many social media sites have a "pop up notification" setting for new messages. If this is a distraction, do not use it. You are the boss, so you do what works best for you.

WEEKLY

- Create a new blog post.
- Ping and social bookmark the post and blog.
- Check stats on blog and Google Analytics.
- Scan Google Alerts.
- Read and research saved information from email files.
- Participate in discussions.

MONTHLY

- Find new Twitter followers. I use Twellow (similar to the yellow pages in the phone book).

- Research and join new groups in the main social media networks.
- Monitor the month and make changes where needed to suit your lifestyle schedule.
- Invite one to three new bloggers who target the same audience and schedule them to post on your blog. This is also a good time for you to request others to consider allowing you to be a guest blogger.
- Recheck/update profile and settings. (Note: really get into the skeleton or account settings of each social media site. For example: Under "Notifications," check to see what selections are checked. Eliminating unwanted notifications will mean fewer emails automatically going into your Inbox, which will save you time in the long run.)

Managing social media activities requires an individualized approach —what works for me may not work for you, and vice versa. What remains the same for all of us is the action of planning—how are you going to manage or balance your social media activities for the day, the week, and the month? We all have to plan in accordance with our own individual schedules. What I have listed are only suggestions. After you begin implementing your own plan, there will be no reason for you to be intimidated. You are your own boss.

Managing Twitter

Tip #1: Tweetdeck – Syndicates the 140-character message automatically into status updates in Facebook, LinkedIn, and MySpace. Also categorizes incoming tweets so you can just glance down and catch the ones that pertain to you. (Note: Hashtags # is a form of categorizing. If you see hashtags like "#Business" or "#mktg," then this tweet is for the attention of business people and marketers. If there is a topic of interest, perhaps where your audience would go, you can create a search column using the related hashtags, catching and managing your tweets that way, too.

Tip #2: Twuffer – Allows scheduled tweets to automatically post during daily, weekly, and monthly sessions.

Tip #3: Ping.fm – A huge time saver that allows you to update dozens of social media sites in one click.

Minimize Time - Maximize Online Presence

*Y*ou have only so much time and want to connect with the most people possible during that time. Now is not the time to stress, but to know you can *conquer all obstacles* by following these solutions to maintaining social media presence.

Build Relationships

Create maximum presence by focusing on the four main social media sites of today:

1.   **Facebook** – In May 2011, there were more than 713 million unique visitors to Facebook worldwide. Of those, 140 million were from the United States. Facebook accounts for 55% of all social site visits and 40% of daily web traffic worldwide. Facebook's audience is about 50-50 male and female.

2.   **Linkedin** – More than 101 million users worldwide, with almost half in the U.S. LinkedIn members are 41% female and 59% male.

3.   **Twitter** – Twitter boasts 200 million users and 350 billion tweets per day. In June 2011, there were 400 million unique visitors per month flocking to Twitter.com.

4.   **Google+** – Google recently released their **Google+ social site**, and some experts speculate that Twitter's popularity may be short lived. Google+ has a Twitter-like "following," rather than a Facebook-like "friending," which means you can follow anyone without his or her permission. While Google+ will soon do all the things Twitter does, Twitter can't support a long list of the things Google+ supports. Keep your eye on Google+.

> *"The big thing I like about Google+ is the PEOPLE on Google+. Everyone is really good at sharing, chatting and helping. I've done experiments on Google+, Twitter, and Facebook where I posted the same question. On Twitter I had 5 responses, on Facebook 0, and on Google+ 26. The quality of those conversations is a lot better, too."*
>
> —Brian Knight, Co-Founder of Premium Promotional Services

How do I promote my business, books, or products?

There is no need to learn new techniques for each of the social media sites. All of them can be handled the same way!

Build Relationships Using These Seven Techniques:

1. **Start Discussions**
    A. Search for groups and join them. For example, if I wrote about promotional tips, I would look for a marketer or author group, and if my practice were very specific such as "blogging tips," I would look for blogger groups and retailers or vendors.
    B. Join the group and await approval from the group administrator.
    C. Once your request is approved, start to read. After you are comfortable with this group, start to post articles, questions or whatever.

2. **Share News**
    A. **Facebook** – Shorten the announcement with abbreviated (bit.ly) link into the status updates.
    B. **LinkedIn** – Once you are a group member, "click" on Submit News and share your blog posts with the entire group.
    C. **Twitter** – Abbreviate the announcement to less than 140 characters. Use hashtags, your twitter name, the link, and the main title for the announcement

3. **Complete your profile**
    Include a photo and very short bio, with a link (if possible).

4. **Answer Questions**
    Prove yourself as an expert. Be a compassionate giver. Show that you are offering unconditional friendship.

5. **Be Proactive**
    Search for those with similar interests, and add them to your network/friend/follower list.

6. **Get Recommendations or Referrals**
    Viral promotion is so powerful.

7. **Help Others**
    Show others you are there for them and you're an expert. The solution to maximizing online social media presence in a minimal amount of

time is to focus on the three top social media sites. Prove that YOU can make a presence and form relationships by following these seven techniques for building relationships.

Syndication – Social Network Sites

I giggle with delight when someone says to me: "You're everywhere!" The secret to massive exposure in my targeted audience is web syndication—posting information once with the ability for this same message to broadcast into other social networks. The wonderful news is … YOU can do magic, too. You can *conquer all obstacles*.

There are many social networks that have climbed on board to help us out. To check for these valuable tools, go into your SETTINGS and search for FEEDS or RSS SETTINGS.

To grab your feeds from your blog, go into FEEDBURNER and click on your site title. At the top, you'll see EDIT FEED DETAILS; click on that and copy ORIGINAL FEED and FEED ADDRESS. This is the RSS FEED needed for your social network site's information.

Performing this trick is like waving the wand. And these downloads are all FREE! Here are the top social network sites I use to syndicate my information:

1. **TWITTER – TWEETDECK**
    Add Twitter status updates and syndicate into Facebook, LinkedIn, and MySpace in THREE CLICKS.

2. **LINKEDIN**
    Go into SETTINGS – click TWITTER and RSS FEEDS. If your blog is created in Wordpress, each post will automatically show up on your profile page. Add updated status, and these will automatically syndicate into Twitter.

The next time someone asks you, "How do you manage to have all that time and energy to be everywhere online," it will be your turn to chuckle. You may even want to answer, "It's magic."

Making the Switch

*D*o you still comment on other blogs, network, and spend time on chat lines like you did in the past? The idea of networking and being sociable will remain strong in my veins. After all, the foundation to "promotion" is establishing relationships. Yet, as time goes by, I have noticed I'm dedicating less time to the faucets in my life that used to be my one and only passion.

So, my answer is "no."

For some reason, I am spending more time on the content (process) and focusing more on the result (production) of my blog.

When did my posts become more important than interacting with others? And why did this happen?

1. **There has been a switch in momentum.**

   It may not be wrong, but a person must self-evaluate the change. Are there more strengths or positives resulting? Has the pendulum swung too far in the other direction?

2. **The cost of time spent on interacting has become too high.**

   There is only so much time in the twenty-four hour cycle, and it must be divided among the tasks at hand. Evaluating the actions and determining the results will dictate the direction you need to take. This will produce the highest yields. Carefully managing your day will result in making the most of the hours you have available. Periodically, re-evaluate where you are. Ask yourself:

   ### *Today, where can I connect with the most people?*

   This will answer your question as to how you should spend most of your time. Effective time management of your day will produce a larger following.

Reaching Your Goal

―❦―

SUCCESS, HERE I COME!

How to Increase Your Success through Online Marketing

WHAT?
Sure, your first impulse or expectation in Internet marketing may be the ultimate dream of getting rich selling your product(s), but perhaps you should be seeing the full picture and consider your hard earned energy. **Embracing opportunities** will increase success.

WHERE?
Network through the top four high traffic media sites: Facebook, LinkedIn, Google+, and Twitter. Also, Goodreads is an excellent media site for authors and readers.

HOW?
1. **Create a complete profile** – Include functional links that will lead the viewer back to the site where your products are sold.
2. **Join groups** – Where is your target audience? Who will be interested in purchasing your product(s) or services? Type those keywords into the search box.
3. **Authentically connect with others** – Participating effectively will establish your presence, create relationships, and increase followers. Contribute to discussions, share content, support others, and provide answers or direction. Stay positive.
4. **Leave your signature (with a link) wherever you can.**
5. **Start your own group** – Contribute bits of your posts (with a link

back to your blog), and then start to invite friends. This will establish a ready-made database; you can broadcast messages to many with only one click.

6.   **Create a blog** – Providing valuable content will attract viewers and have them coming back for more.

WHY?

You can look forward to:

DEFINED PURPOSE – Immediate interaction with a community of similar-minded folks. An excellent resource base just waiting to support your journey and answer any question. A sense of belonging and purpose.

SALES – Massive exposure in front of potential buyers or clients—a greater chance to sell your products.

GENUINE REFERRAL SOURCES – Viral promotion is powerful! One voice can soon escalate to multiples. It's the "breeding of the bunnies" that should be the focus. Selling your product is good, but can you imagine having a trusted friend spreading the news and having their friends sharing who you are and what you have to sell? There's nothing better than referrals and personal testimonies. Just think of the last time a friend (a personal connection) told you to buy something versus buying something off the rack. There's really no comparison.

Online marketing or creating an Internet presence WILL create MANY opportunities and INCREASE your success.

The Secret to Success is Facebook

*D*o you want greater sales? Today, Facebook is the #1 social media site on the net. Every morning, I post links about marketing tips, new reviews, and interviews. I post updated social status information about my personal life—short, snappy notes to keep my followers up to date and interested.

FACT: *As of late 2011, Facebook has reached more than 750 million users in the world.*[†]

How do I direct my viewers from Facebook back to my site where my products are sold?

1. **Know your audience** – To get attention and keep your audience from leaving never to return, create unique pages that are on topics of interest. Put yourself in their shoes and know what interests them.

FACT: *Women over age 45 and making over 60K annually make up the majority of the Facebook audience. 53% have children.*[†]

Fill your feature page with pictures, podcasts, and valuable content or resource materials—topics suited to the majority of the Facebook audience.

The link I use takes viewers back to my site where my products are sold.

2. **Be genuine, show your knowledge, and show interest** – Again, think of where your audience will hang out on Facebook. Join Facebook group pages. Engage your audience by participating in discussions. Leave comments, ask questions, and respond to concerns. Be fun. Click the LIKE (thumbs-up) button to show interest in their links and posts.

3. **Promote your Facebook Business Pages and Facebook Group** – Don't forget to invite others to your business page by leaving a functioning link at the bottom of your blog posts or as part of your signature.

If your goal is to sell a product online, ignore the negativity from the media about Facebook. If you have previously been opposed to Facebook, perhaps it's time to change your mind. As of late 2011, Facebook has reached 750 million users in the world. How can you afford NOT to be there?

[†] http://en.wikipedia.org/wiki/Facebook_statistics

12 Steps to Avoid Being Anonymous

*H*ave you ever felt like you must have "Anonymous" stamped on your forehead? Have you grumbled about marketing, been disappointed in your sales, and wanted to give-up?

Sometimes it takes "hitting the wall" before we seek recovery. The following *12 Steps[†] to Avoid Being Anonymous* will help pull you off the wall and back onto the road to success.

12 Steps to Avoid Being Anonymous

1. *Admitted that I was powerless over consumers, that my marketing endeavors had become fruitless and unmanageable.*

   No matter how much I market, there are no guarantees for the exact number of sales. Yet, the more exposure I have, the greater my chance of success and increased sales.

2. *Came to believe that I needed help, and learning from my fellow marketers could restore me to sanity.*

   Going solo while marketing on the Internet exhausts my energy. Reaching out to other experts in my field or my targeted audience and linking our sites, giving guest posts, and accepting interviews will speed the spread of my platform.

3. *Made a decision to let go of unrealistic expectations and to write blog posts according to my understanding.*

   Setting myself up for unrealistic expectations only leads to terrible results and even a sense of failure. Planning is okay. So I will toss out my fears and post my articles. I will be ready to write, write, and write some more.

4. *Made a searching and fearless inventory of the Internet resources.*

   I will find my area of expertise and hone in on the experts. I have given myself permission to surf the net to find them.

5. *Admitted to my fellow marketers, to myself, and to my viewers the exact nature of my marketing plans.*

   Formality in sharing my knowledge may be appreciated, but may

---

[†]Not affiliated with and no association to Alcoholics Anonymous or any of their organizations.

leave the viewers searching elsewhere for information that is easier to understand and more entertaining. I have learned that mixing formality with conversational writing will keep my readers coming back. Showing flaws will portray realism. I will share my true voice.

6. *Became entirely ready to have my fans remove all the awful feelings of past rejections.*

    Reasons why I shut down and suddenly go into writer's block:

    1. Focusing on the negative.
    2. Expectations not being met – sales down.
    3. Dwelling on a disappointing outcome.

    Using praise from my fans can bring me up and activate the muse. I can change my attitude and focus. No longer do I care about my sales; instead, I really care about my fans and the desire to support my fellow marketers.

7. *Humbly asked viewers to keep coming back.*
    Spam is just wrong. Genuinely giving great content and showing that I need them work to my benefit.

8. *Made a list of all promotional tactics I had used in the past and became willing to make improvements to them all.*
    Using the successful promotional techniques I used a year ago may not work today. Even yesterday's tactics may not work anymore. To accept this society as a changing entity will help take the focus off my faults or mishaps and place them more on the reasons for change.

9. *Made direct updates to such marketing tactics, except when to do so would drive us to insanity.*
    Again, what worked yesterday may not work today. I can prepare for change. I can be constantly searching out new methods. I will work this daily education into my day planner.

10. *Continued to evaluate, and when we were receiving less hits promptly acknowledged it.*
    I see rises and falls, ups and downs. I can prepare for the roller coaster by spreading my abilities and gifts. *For example:* If one of my blog posts has a drop in hits (according to the Google Analytics), I will then enter the social media sites and help a fellow marketer with a marketing dilemma. I cannot expect my stats to always rise on a high

peak, so when the hits decrease, I have to plan for an alternative means of accomplishment.

11. *Sought through inspirational experts to improve my marketing plan for consumers, as I understand them, hoping only for knowledge of their purchasing buttons and the power to carry that out.*

Switching roles from businessperson to artist and back again is quite a feat. Now you must be a marketer, a publicist, and quite often a distributor in order to sell your goods. As entrepreneurs and business men and women, we have accepted that we have to wear many hats to perform the end results—sales. The blessing is the Internet. The unbelievable amount of information and experts are now captured with a few clicks on a keyboard.

12. *Having had remarkable ideas as the result of these resources, I tried to carry this knowledge to fellow marketers and to practice these marketing tips in all our affairs.*

The sheer bulk of all the information on the Internet can be overwhelming. I do have the ability to scan. I am literate—a gift to many in this world. I climb higher and sell more by gathering together with others. Team work is the answer, and there are many willing teammates out in cyberspace.

It works if you work it.

YOU ARE WORTH IT!

Turning An Audience into Followers, fans & friends

*T*he other day, someone asked me why their products weren't selling. She said she had lots of hits on her blog, and she had a huge following.

Don't let the numbers fool you!

I asked her if her audience was made up of **followers** or **fans** and if she considered herself a loyal **friend** to others.

There is a difference. I tell clients that first you will have an audience, then your audience will turn into followers, and finally, these folks will become your fans. It is a slow process at first, but necessary to selling products online. Like the proverbial snowball rolling down a hill, however, once started it grows bigger and bigger.

> ### *A Loyal and Trusting Relationship ...*
> ### *The cost is nothing ... the result is priceless!*

How to Turn Your Audience Into Loyal Fans

- **Make an impression** – Be supportive and give away amazing content that will help others—unconditionally! Be proactive, genuine, expecting nothing in return.

- **Prove You're an Expert** – Don't keep secrets. What I learn from other marketers and bloggers, I pass on as brief informative posts. When I am researching and come across a post that makes me gasp and say, "Now that's just way too cool," chances are, others will feel the same. That is the content I need to share.

- **Solve Problems** – Comment and give solutions in social media <u>forums</u> or groups. There will be others with the same problem. I provide not only the answer, but the shortest possible route. Simplicity and instant

---

Forums: A place or community within a social network site where people "hang-out." The group members share similar interests and support one another through discussions or question and answer techniques.

solutions are what others want. Cut the fluff and chop the lengthy explanations.

- **Show You're Human** – Write articles with a mixture of formality and conversation. I make confessions all the time. I'm not afraid to share my flaws and areas of weakness, and even chuckle (LOL) along with others. Relating to others personally will tighten the bond into a trusting relationship.

- **Give** – The best gift you can give others is your time. Take the time to converse one-on-one. I produce and host a BlogTalkRadio (BTR) show called "Authors Articulating." My motive is pure and simple: I want to help others. I take the time to pre- and post-promote, register and produce the show, and chat with my guest. The cost for them is nothing. The results for both of us is priceless—a loyal and trusting relationship.

How does this sell more products online?

- **Readers will absorb your comments and click on your name**—a link leading them back to your profile/site where your products are sold. They will share with others what they have learned. Viral promotion is so, so powerful.

- **Fans are true friends.** Through thick and thin, they will loyally follow, purchase your products, and help spread the word to others.

Scams – Beware of the Swarming Sharks

*T*rust takes a long time to gain and a second to lose. I know, I've been burned. Thankfully, I turned to the Internet and Googled myself silly. While on the World Wide Web (www), I discovered there are many of us who are supportive and in the same boat.

What a wonderful feeling to belong in a community of caring people. Unfortunately, there are those who have not been so lucky. They have been a victim of a scammer. Some have lost thousands of dollars and had their dreams crushed.

In my prior profession, I was often accused of being too compassionate. I admit that I took my work home with me and let the sorrows of others absorb through my skin and sink deep into my veins. I defended my friends, and as a teacher, I wanted to take many of those students home with me, those whom I knew were living in bad situations. Gosh, it's sad ...

Today, I feel the same. I want to help defend my fellow entrepreneurs and Internet marketers. An invisible force pulls me forward to warn you about the sharks swarming just above your head, ready to dive for the kill.

Maybe you have decided you would rather run your business and leave the marketing to someone who has the time, knowledge, and ability to promote you and your goods. I cannot say I blame you. Promoting is a full time job. And if you're anything like me, having trouble shifting from managing your business, produced from one hemisphere of the brain, to the business of selling, the other hemisphere of the brain, you may not have any other choice. You will either have to hire someone to do your Internet marketing, or you will have to stop managing and learn this new avenue.

Before you decide on hiring someone to provide promotional services of any kind, do your homework. Ask for referrals from past clients of the business. Watch for any false phrases.

Do not be fresh bait for these phrases:

- **"We can guarantee sales"** – No one can guarantee sales. There are too many variables that determine success, too many circumstances that can erupt that are out of the marketer's control.

Example: A product's worth is subjective in the eyes of others. Will your product appeal to the majority of an audience? Remember, what you like doesn't dictate what everyone else likes. Even a product name or title can sometimes make or break a few sales.

Example: An economic crash or boom can cause market fluctuations.

> *Creating a platform, targeting the right audience, building relationships with potential purchasers, generating traffic to the site where your products are sold, will increase the chances of the successful sale of your goods, but there are still no guarantees in regards to sales, and no promotional manager or marketer should ever make that promise.*

- **"We can get you into the top search engines"** – Again, this is a false statement. There are too many active crawlers that constantly hoist new material up and down within seconds.

> *Establishing internal and external links will activate webcrawlers to raise your ranks in the search engines, but it is highly unlikely that you and your products will be placed at the top right away. Even if you make it to the top, you will be there for only a second, and then the shift continues.*

- **"We can get you media exposure now"** – Wrong! Promotion takes time. Building a platform takes time. There is a lot of competition out there. A promotional manager must create a profile that stands out from the rest, draws the attention of viewers, establishes a trusting relationship with the followers, then navigates the fans to the purchase button. This does not happen overnight. Marketing for others takes dedication and commitment from an honest person. Selling a product takes hard work and even a little luck.

No matter how good something sounds, take a deep breath and step back. Take the time needed to research and inquire.

Scare away the predators by not supplying them with bait. Sharks will not stick around if there is no food to eat.

No More fear

I shared previously that one of my biggest fears in life is getting lost. My palms get sweaty just thinking about it. Unfortunately, having no sense of direction is not only a daunting fear for many entrepreneurs and marketers, but it can cause one to feel completely lost. This is a reality.

Fear no more. There is a straight, clear path to promoting your business and your products. To *conquer all obstacles* is to have **direction**.

All you have to do is devise a specific plan and discover your balance.

It's very important that you plan, but be sure to set realistic expectations. Expecting an unrealistic outcome can bring discouragement. Enjoy the process, and the result is a bonus.

Yes, plan, and write it down. Don't keep it all in your head. A visual measurement of your progress is proven to boost morale and will bring an encouraging sense of accomplishment.

Answer the five "Ws," and your plan is set in motion.

The Five Ws—The Marketing Plan

Who, What, When, Where, and we know Why!

1. *Who?* **AUDIENCE** – Who will be interested in your product(s)?

2. *What?* **SERVICES** – What services will generate the most exposure— Platforms, Reviews, Interviews, Virtual Tours, Blog or Website Redesign?

3. *When?* **TIME** – When are you going to find the time to contact ALL of your waiting fans and followers?

4. *Where?* **NETWORK** – Where are you going to display your profile and products?

5. *Why?* **REWARDS** – There must be a win-win for both the buyer and the seller.

Discovering the Balance

Too many times, there is temptation to jump to the last step in the marketing plan first. We want to know **where** to go before addressing the **who**, **what**, and **when**. Your marketing plan is not the place to take short cuts. Skipping steps will only result in utter confusion or wasted time marketing in the wrong places.

Discover a balance. **Where** to promote will come automatically after you have gone through the progressive steps of planning and completing the **who**, **what**, and **when**.

WHO ...
- Search for followers in a variety of areas. (Social Media Networks—Facebook, LinkedIn, and Twitter.)
- Network in many different groups. Join discussions, and leave your brand/signature.
- Promote locally (seminars, presentations, etc.), and reach out through the Internet.
- Vary your presentation techniques to fit the needs of each individual. Who you are chatting with will determine the formality of the chat/ conversation.

WHAT ...
- Meet the needs of your viewers by selecting as many services as possible. (Review Services in #2 above.)
- Sprinkle each service throughout the networks in a press release format.
- Soon after the initial meeting, introduce your product(s). (Many viewers will already be asking.) But, don't push the sale yet. Be patient, the viewers are now hooked.
- Sprinkle in a little few more services. No ... don't push yet ...

WHEN ...
- Schedule your day by dividing the clock. Keep track of how you spend your time and evaluate. Are you getting what you planned finished? If the answer is no, ask yourself why.
- The next day, try rearranging your priorities. What you did not complete yesterday will fit in today.

WHERE ...
- After you peg *who* your target audience is, *what* services you are sprinkling into the market, and *when* the amount of time will be allotted to each group, the *where* is simple.
- Now you can sell your product(s). Set the hook, and reel in your fans. Push hard, be strong, and don't hold anything back.

WHY ...

- Give your fans what they want—good products that meet a need, and you will be rewarded. It's a win-win situation. I like that, and look ... my palms are dry.

You can *conquer all obstacles* by following a plan of action, a marketing plan using the Five-Ws. The secret in selling your goods is knowing **who** to address, **what** services or tactics work, **when** to set the hook and start reeling in the fans, and **where** all the action takes place. Not many people like a pushy salesperson, nor do they like to be left in limbo. It is up to you to find that balance.

Trust your instincts by really listening to your viewers.

✑

Whether you are a novice or an expert, you can save time and energy when marketing your products. The ideas, directions, and tips in this book will create massive exposure and drive traffic to the site where your products are sold.

You CAN *conquer all obstacles*.

—Jo-Anne Vandermeulen

Glossary

———— ❦ ————

POPULAR INTERNET TERMS

Alerts (Google): A service offered by Google, the search engine company, that notifies users when content from news, web, blogs, videos, or other groups matches search terms that have been pre-selected by the user in the Google Alerts service.

Address (Web): The URL or location of a site on the Internet. The address bar is usually found at the top of your browser and begins with http://.

Badge: A small graphic icon displayed on a blog or personal profile on social media sites that identifies you. Most badges encourage readers and followers to download and display their badge and to link back.

Bit.ly: A utility that allows users to shorten the length of a URL and then track the resulting usage.

Blog: An interactive Internet site. A term shortened from "weblog," a type of website for journaling in chronological order with newest posts first, usually by one person, with the option of allowing Comments from readers.

Blogger: Someone who makes posts to a blog, or Blogger.com.

Blogging: Making a post to a blog.

Blog Pages: Multiple pages of a blog site. Clicking on the tabs (usually found at the top of the pages), will direct the viewer to different pages. Common pages include: Home, Bio, About, Reviews, Contact.

Blog Platform: The software used to create blogs, the most popular being Blogger and Wordpress.

Blogroll: A list of other blog sites that are recommended by the blogger, usually placed in the sidebar.

Cyberspace: The virtual world of computers and their networks—Internet, World Wide Web or www.

Dashboard: An interactive user interface that organizes and presents information in a way that is easy to read and manipulate. The skeleton of your blog—the place to design, add or move widgets, change settings and appearance, include media, and store stats.

Database: A collection of related data organized for easy access, such as a collection of email addresses.

E-Book: An electronic book, a digital file that readers can download from the Internet and read on a computer or a handheld device.

Editor: The person who puts a literary work into acceptable form with accurate syntax, grammar, spelling, and punctuation. Also, one who manages the editorial process.

Forums: A place or community within a social network site where people "hang-out." The group members share similar interests and support one another through discussions or question and answer techniques.

Functioning Link: When a link works to connect to another URL (internal page or external site). Ideally, that external site connects back with yours, so that you are sharing traffic.

Hashtags: Indicated by the # symbol followed by a keyword or topic that categorizes Twitter messages. For example: If I'm tweeting about Internet Marketing, I would add the following hashtags: #mktg, #business, #authors.

Home Page: The landing page, feature, or first page the viewer sees when arriving at your blog or website. New blog posts will appear here, along with the generic sidebar(s) as seen on all your additional pages.

Hook: The first sentence that grabs a reader's attention.

HTML: HyperText Markup Language, the predominant computer language (code) for building web pages.

Keywords or Phrases: A blend of words used in your title and content depicting the content. The purpose of using keywords and key phrases is to aid the search engines in matching information that is typed into a browser search bar with information in the search engine databases.

Keywords or Tags: A word or phrase that BEST describes the subject or article. When searching for an article, what you would type in the search engine to find it.

Kindle: Amazon's wireless e-book reader.

KISS: An acronym for "Keep It Simple, Sweetie," or Silly, or Stupid.

Links: A highlighted or activated word, phrase, or address that, when clicked, will direct the viewer to another URL or site.

Long-Tailed Keywords: A combination of words making up a keyword phrase that helps narrow the selection category in a search engine.

Lurker: A person who reads blog discussions but never comments.

MetaTags: A tag embedded in HTML code to describe a site's content and provide keywords to inform web crawlers about your page.

Massive Exposure: Appearance in many places, expanding your Network.

Niche: A certain interest group toward whom you will focus your efforts. Your area of expertise. Thoughts should come easy when you're writing about your passion.

Page Rank: Indicates the page on which your link or site shows up in Search Results. The goal is to be on the first page.

Ping: A utility used to test the delay between or to generate a response from one computer to another on a network or the Internet.

Pingbacks: A notification that another blogger on the Internet linked to one of your posts in their post. It shows up as a comment in your post and includes a link back to their post where you can approve, delete, or spam the pingback.

Pitch: A short paragraph or verbal conversation that is intended to hook buyers for the product(s) you are hoping to sell.

Platform: Where you tell the world about yourself and your products or services. Building a personal, reputable identity is essential in Internet marketing. Stand out from the rest.

Post: An entry made to a blog.

Profile: The personal information about yourself that you provide during registration.

RSS Badge: A pagelet that allows visitors to easily find and subscribe to your site's RSS feed.

RSS Feed: Rich Site Summary, commonly called Really Simple Syndication, is a format for delivering regularly changing web content.

Search Engines: A program for the retrieval of data, files, or documents from a database or the Internet. You can find others, answers, and/or products. Examples of the top three search engines include: Google, Bing, and Yahoo. Approximate Market Share: Google–79.19%, Bing–9.03%, Yahoo–8.79%, Ask–1.66%, AOL–1.32%.

SEO: Search Engine Optimization. A strategy used to boost your site higher in the Search Engine Page Rank.

SEO Strategies: Strategies for boosting your Page Rank include: adding keywords or tags to each post, registering your site with the top search engines, pinging each new post, adding your link with the bookmarking services, such as Digg, StumbleUpon, and Delicious.

Sidebar: The smaller columns to the left and/or right of the main center column on a blog page. Typically, widgets and a variety of links and information of the blogger's choice are added to the sidebars.

Signature Block: Up to 4 lines stating the name, label of expertise, product name, and site address. Commonly used at the bottom of email messages. Not the same as a digital signature that is encrypted to provide verifiable proof of authorship.

Social Bookmarks: A method that stores and organizes keywords or tags to ensure optimized search engine results.

Social Networking: Developing relationships by conversation, whether in person or online, that grows into a trusting bond through interactive connection—becoming friends.

Social Network Sites: A community on the Internet where individuals register to become members, supply their profiles, accept and send friend requests to gather their own following or fans. Popular social network sites today are Facebook, Twitter, and LinkedIn.

Spamming: Unsolicited commercial messages sent via email, or forwarded emails.

Stats: Short for "statistics." Stats show the number of visitors, their locations, how they got there, and how long they spent on each page.

Subscribe: A viewer who wishes to receive notification via email of new posts. This will also allow the blogger to attain email addresses. A collection of these email addresses is called a "database."

Tags: A keyword or term associated with or assigned to a post or piece of information. Tags make it easier for search engines to find you.

Target Your Audience: Focus your energy toward viewers who may be interested in your product (gathering a following).

Traffic: The number of visitors to a blog or website. Your audience, followers, or fans who travel around your site clicking on the links to read more about you or your products. To determine the size of your traffic, go to your stats page.

Tweet: A maximum 140-character post or status update on Twitter. Precise presentation packed with information. Note: Always include the link. Again, this will drive traffic to you and your product(s). Here's a recent example of a Tweet:

#business #authors #blogtalkradio with @conquerall MARK YOUR CALENDARS! 24/10/2011 21:00 "INTERNET MARKETING MADE EASY"!

Twitter Name: Indicated by the @ symbol followed by a username that identifies you. This will help lurkers to use your tweet name and direct others back to your twitter profile. For example: My twitter name is @conquerall.

URL: Uniform Resource Locator, the "address" of a web page. The link to your site (begins with http://) found at the top of your browser.

Viral Promotion: Sharing information you've seen with others by talking or writing. A form of recommendation.

Web Crawler: A computer program that browses the World Wide Web creating a copy of all the visited pages for later processing by search engines. This new content will boost you higher in the Search Engines. This strategy is called Search Engine Optimization (SEO). For example, being page ranked 3 means that the viewer will only need to scroll to page 3 to find you—a far cry from the thousands of pages that exist.

Widgets: Small programs you can add to your website or blog; includes icons, pull-down menus, buttons, selection boxes, progress indicators, on-off checkmarks, scroll bars, windows, window edges (that let you resize the window), toggle buttons, forms, and many other devices for displaying information and for inviting, accepting, and responding to user actions. Widgets are usually found on blog sidebars. There are hundreds of widgets to choose from. These widgets dress or add personality to your blog. For example, a widget will allow you to add images or pictures.

About the Author

*J*O-ANNE VANDERMEULEN graduated from the University of Saskatchewan with a degree in Education and a major in English Literature. For 20 years, she enjoyed a full life raising her two daughters as a single mom and working as a full-time teacher. That left little time for fulfilling her lifelong dream of writing.

At the age of forty-two, Jo-Anne's life drastically changed. She was diagnosed with a medical illness that sent her home from the classroom.

Determined not to let this devastation ruin her life, she used the unplanned turn of events as an opportunity to fulfill her dream. In just seventeen days, Jo-Anne wrote her first novel, a story that was unbelievably self healing.

Since that time, Jo-Anne's second book, a romantic thriller titled *Conquer All Obstacles,* has been published. She has welcomed her new career, the journey to publication, while developing an expertise in the promotional industry. Now having the time to pursue her writing and develop her goals, she has:

- produced four completed novels in addition to this non-fiction resource you are presently reading, *Internet Marketing Made Easy,* which was pre-requested by thousands of followers. Her previous book, *Premium Promotional Tips for Writers,* earned many 5-star reviews.

The first book Jo-Anne wrote is still awaiting publication, but her second fiction novel, *Conquer All Obstacles,* was published and released in September 2009. It is getting rave reviews;

- created an author platform—belonging to over 30 social media networks where her audience networks through her two blogs, "Free Marketing Tips for Writers" and "Journey to Publication";
- gained a wealth of experience through attending writing conferences, participating in online workshops, gaining membership in several writing associations, and meeting publishers to pitch her first book.

Jo-Anne soon discovered that the writing and publishing journey does not stop there. After diving into online support groups and following professional bloggers, she learned the skills and techniques to successfully promote and market books and other goods. Her desire to help others led her to share the new information she had found in the form of posts in her "Free Marketing Tips" blog. Not long after, her fellow writers recognized her expertise and began to contact her asking to utilize her promotional services.

Yes, Jo-Anne discovered her new niche in life.

The demand for Jo-Anne's marketing and promotional services rapidly grew. Thousands of authors and entrepreneurs requested her services. A new opportunity knocked, and the door opened. All she had to do was walk through.

PREMIUM PROMOTIONAL SERVICES: *You Create – We Promote* was born—a new venture that is successfully filling the demanding gap for many people wanting to market via the Internet. Her business offers the services necessary to target audiences, create massive exposure, and drive traffic back to the clients' sites where their products are sold. See endorsements at:

www.premiumpromotions.biz

New media opportunities led Jo-Anne to produce and host a weekly live Internet radio show called "Authors Articulating." This BlogTalkRadio show hosts both renowned guests and aspiring authors in an energetic podcast where they and Jo-Anne discuss various promotional and writing topics, and listeners are encouraged to interact, deliver their platforms, and pitch their books.

Along with her business partner, Brian Knight, Jo-Anne states, "Together, we have our hearts set on helping people. We care!" She often says that "supporting others comes naturally." Her name and brand, "Conquer All Obstacles," can be seen buzzing through many social media sites as she answers questions and responds to calls for assistance.

"You can turn devastations or unplanned events into opportunities," she beams to anyone who will listen. She has proven that *conquering all obstacles* is possible as she continues to encourage fellow writers, marketers, entrepreneurs, and her followers that they, too, can overcome life's unexpected tragedies.

From her home in British Columbia, Jo-Anne is happily living her dream come true with her furry housemate, Oscar. She is currently promoting her new books and those of her clients while she continues to fulfill her lifelong dream of writing.

Books by Jo-Anne Vandermeulen

Conquer All Obstacles

Premium Promotional Tips for Writers

Internet Marketing Made Easy

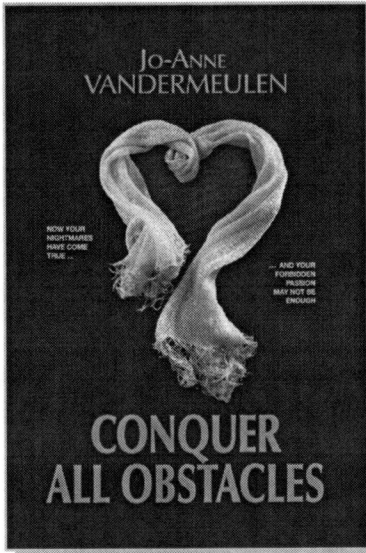

JO-ANNE VANDERMEULEN

Founder, Owner and Marketeer of
PREMIUM PROMOTIONAL SERVICES
You Create – We Promote
www.premiumpromotions.biz

Online Social Media and Marketing Expert
FREE MARKETING TIPS
www.joconquerobstacles.com

Produces and Hosts a Live Radio Show
AUTHORS ARTICULATING
www.blogtalkradio.com/prempromotions

Nonfiction and Fiction Author
• *CONQUER ALL OBSTACLES* (Suspense/Romance)
• *PREMIUM PROMOTIONAL TIPS FOR WRITERS*
(Non-fiction/Resource)

Visit Her Personal Sites
Journey to Publication – www.joconquerall.com
Conquer All Obstacles – www.joconquerobstacles.com

Jo-Anne welcomes followers at:
www.facebook.com/joanne.vandermeulen
(or any of her business pages)
www.twitter.com/conquerall

CPSIA information can be obtained at www.ICGtesting.com
Printed in the USA
LVOW030622301211

261636LV00005B/2/P